A CELTIC LITURGY
for EVERY SEASON

ELIZABETH LOVETT GROVER

∞ INFINITY
PUBLISHING

ISBN 978-0-7414-8245-7   Paperback
ISBN 978-0-7414-8246-4   eBook

Printed in the United States of America

Published February 2013

INFINITY PUBLISHING
1094 New DeHaven Street, Suite 100
West Conshohocken, PA 19428-2713
Toll-free (877) BUY BOOK
Local Phone (610) 941-9999
Fax (610) 941-9959
Info@buybooksontheweb.com
www.buybooksontheweb.com

Acknowledgements

I would like to thank all the throngs of folk whose thoughts and beliefs contributed to this book, but especially the following: The Rt. Rev. Martin Townsend and the Rev. Dr. John Philip Newell (for inspiration); the Rev. Bruce Freeman and the Rev. Charlie Brumbaugh (for encouragement); the Rev. Andrew MacAoidh Jergens, the Rev. Nancy Hopkins-Greene, and Juliette Stuard (for editorial advice and assistance); and my husband John Grover (for musical inspiration and loving support).

Table of Contents

Introduction

In recent years there has been a resurgence of interest in
the traditions and spirituality that are distinct to the Celtic
expression of Christianity. Although some renewal has
taken place in Celtic lands (such as the Iona Community in
Scotland), the trend is not confined to the borders of areas
settled by Celtic peoples. In the twenty-first century, a
number of American churches – especially Episcopal
churches – have started offering a worship service
described as "Celtic." The liturgies offered in this book
provide resources for such a service.

A Brief Look at Celtic Christianity

Who were the Celts?

The history of the Christian church includes the story of
Christianity in what is now Great Britain and Ireland. The
peoples known as the Celts came to these isles from Europe
and practiced their own religion before Christianity was
introduced. The Insular Celtic languages spoken at that
time were of two distinct (though related) language
families – the Brythonic (in what is now England, Wales and
Southern Scotland) and the Goidelic (in Ireland, Western
Scotland and the Isle of Man). The Brythonic Celts were
conquered by the Romans in the first century A.D., but the
Goidelic Celts were not. This led to a differentiation in the
history, culture, and religious practices of each of these
separate sets of peoples.

A separate Celtic tradition

The Romans introduced Britain (and the Brythonic Celts) to
Christianity, but during the Dark Ages, Christianity was only
one of many religions in the region. The Christian faith was
introduced to Ireland in the fifth century, and like the Gaelic
language, was exported from there to parts of Scotland by
Columba and others.

Remnants of Celtic paganism – an active and vital religious
practice – were naturally incorporated into the new faith.
Both the old and the new religions were very focused on a
sense of place and its sacredness. There were a number of
instances of Christian chapels being built on the sites of
former Druidic sanctuaries. The concept of holy places is
important in Celtic thought and is reflected in the Celtic
notion of "thin places."

The isolation of Christianity in Ireland and in rural areas of Wales and Scotland allowed the traditions of these areas to develop separately from Roman or other continental influence. This was exaggerated by the strong tradition of monasticism which kept the church decentralized as well as by the strength of the Celtic oral tradition which discouraged assimilation with more literate influences.

By the end of the sixth century, the views and traditions of the Celtic expression of Christianity and the monasteries where those traditions thrived were under attack from both Rome and Canterbury. Officials of the established church wanted to bring the practices and customs of the Celtic branch of the faith into conformity with and under the authority of the continental Christian Church. At the Synod of Whitby in 664, the Roman Catholic Church and its practices were officially selected and sanctioned over those of the Celtic Christians.

Subsequently, a number of Viking attacks on monasteries, the advent of the Normans and their continental influence, and eventually, Henry VIII's closure of all monasteries disrupted the Christian traditions in Ireland and Scotland quite profoundly. It is significant, however, that the oral traditions remained, and that Celtic expressions of the faith were preserved in poetry and song in such works as *Carmina Gadelica* and *The Religious Songs of Connacht*.

The revival of the ancient Celtic faith

In the late nineteenth and early twentieth centuries, a revival of interest in Celtic ways began with these same two works. Alexander Carmichael in Scotland and Douglas Hyde in Ireland brought the *Carmina* and the *Connacht* respectively to the world's attention. Others including

George MacLeod, founder of the Iona Community, also contributed by taking the old Celtic traditions and perspectives and making them new, relevant, and fresh. Today when many mainstream churches are losing members, the appeal of this ancient, yet seemingly new approach to the Christian life is keeping the faith alive in Celtic lands and around the world.

Features of Celtic theology

What is the nature of Celtic Christianity that make its theology unique and distinct from Roman Catholic Christianity? There are many standard elements of Christian theology that are shared in the Celtic tradition – such as the incarnation, death, and resurrection of Christ. The distinctiveness of the Celtic philosophy is rooted in its focus on the presence of the divine in the physical world. God is experienced in all of creation and therefore in all of nature. This concept leads to other closely related theological notions. If God is in all things, then the natural world is to be celebrated and honored as holy. This extends to every aspect of life, including human life as well. The everyday world is infused with a spiritual presence – even in the most mundane, everyday activities. For example, the ancient Celts had prayers for washing dishes and for drinking beer.

Another set of related concepts was that of holy geography: holy places – earthly sites where the divine seemed particularly present – and thin places – where the sense of a veil between the spiritual and the physical seemed to fade.

If creation is holy, humankind is a part of creation and therefore also holy and sacred. The Celts appreciated the whole of creation and saw humanity as just another kind of creature – not as the rulers of earth. If creation is not only holy but good and humans are part of creation, then humans are basically good. This is a much different focus from the concept of original sin common in Augustinian Roman Christianity. The basic goodness of humans can bring joy – a joy in the acceptance and celebration of God's love for all people. This celebration engenders another Celtic concept – a strong sense of community, because all people together are valued and loved.

The Nature of Celtic Liturgy

Applying Celtic theology

Celtic worship based on these principles – the increased awareness of the presence of God in all things – can bring new life into old liturgical practices. A liturgy in the Celtic tradition should reflect these theological principles. There is a focus on the natural world and a sense of celebration. Often penitential elements are de-emphasized, and the joy of being in God's presence and love is celebrated.

As the natural world and all things physical are celebrated, they are mentioned more often in Celtic theology. Because God's love for all creates a sense of the value of people, the people (i.e. congregation) have a much larger role than in some other liturgies; hence there is often more congregational participation in a Celtic service. In addition, the use of repetition also serves to infuse the Holy Spirit into our very being in a mantra-like technique. These are some of the techniques that can make the Celtic liturgy distinctive and meaningful.

A Holy Eucharist in the Celtic tradition

At the Episcopal Church of the Redeemer in Cincinnati, Ohio, we have been offering a celebration of the "Holy Eucharist in the Celtic tradition" since November, 2005. Originally modeled loosely on a liturgy from the Church of the Holy Communion in Memphis, with additions from some Iona sources, our Celtic service has developed into a thematically focused, contemporary liturgy based on the theology of the ancient Celts enlivened with traditional music. There is a different theme (many based on natural elements) for each season, and these themes of nature change throughout the liturgical year (with a different liturgy for each theme). A few extra adjustments to the liturgical calendar allow us to add even more variety – especially in the long season after Pentecost. We offer two separate Pentecost liturgies – one with the theme of fire and one with the theme of wind.

Crafting a Celtic liturgy

The liturgies have been crafted from a variety of sources. Recent works which have been very important sources are those by two great men of deep spirituality – David Adam and J. Philip Newell. Adam was at one time the vicar on the Holy Island of Lindisfarne, and Newell was at one time the warden of the abbey on the Isle of Iona. Iona and Lindisfarne are two of the most important sites for Celtic Christianity, both historically and currently. The prayers of these and others have been selected and arranged in a sequence that is recognizable to those familiar with today's liturgical traditions – especially the Episcopal Church in the United States. Some ancient Celtic texts are arranged differently, but when trying to reach contemporary audiences, a familiar order of service can make unusual liturgies more accessible.

One result of the rearrangement of liturgical elements is an occasional choppiness to the flow of the liturgy. For this reason transitions have been added. Rubrics with directions have been minimized due to variation in local practice across parishes. Important directions can be added to your own bulletin or can simply be announced. For example, your congregation may want to add (or add more) pauses in the intercessory prayers to allow the people to add their own petitions. Of course, directions regarding standing and sitting or the addition of periods of silence may also vary by local custom.

One issue in crafting a Eucharistic liturgy in the Celtic tradition is that, because the Celtic monastic tradition was rooted in the daily office, it has historically been much less common to find examples of *Eucharistic* liturgies that reflect the Celtic outlook. J. Philip Newell's *An Earthful of Glory* is one exception to this, and is an excellent resource in this process. The Iona Community offers some Eucharistic liturgies as well.

Considerations in Celtic Liturgies

Themes that differentiate these services

A distinctive feature of the compilation offered in this book is the variety of liturgies for different seasons of the liturgical year. The seasonal themes chosen for these liturgies are intended both to reflect Celtic theological principles and to provide a focus – usually on an element of the natural world.

★ Advent: The liturgical year begins with the season in which we prepare for Christmas – Advent; the theme for Advent is sound, as we are waiting and listening for God.

★ The Nativity or Christmastide is a very short season when we focus on the gift of Jesus and our thankfulness for the gift of love.

★ Epiphany: The theme of light for Epiphany is carried through the time after this feast day. It represents the enlightenment of the world with the spreading of the Gospel.

★ Lent: Peace for Lent – the forty days before Easter – focuses on the quiet, contemplative tone of this penitential season.

★ Easter: The creation and the celebration of new growth mark the season of Easter – the season when we celebrate the Resurrection.

★ Pentecost: There are two themes for Pentecost – the wind representing the Holy Spirit as the breath of God and the fire which is the tongue of flame in which the

Holy Spirit arrived on the Day of Pentecost. Since the season after Pentecost is so long, these two options offer a little more variety.

★ All Saints: One additional theme – that of water – brings another opportunity for variety on All Saints' Day in November. We use the water/saints liturgy throughout November even though technically All Saints is just one day and not a season. This theme can be used for baptisms as well.

Music in a Celtic service

At Redeemer most Sundays during the program year, our service is enriched by music provided by our Celtic music ensemble. In different configurations, a variety of instruments including guitar, harp, recorder, flute, violin, hammered dulcimer, concertina and bohdran join in playing traditional tunes from Scotland, Ireland and other Celtic lands. (Other instruments would also serve including piano, oboe, and more.)

There are thousands of Celtic tunes available in the public domain. We don't limit what we play to church music. The prelude, offertory, communion, and postlude pieces are usually instrumental pieces, and it is consistent with Celtic theology that we acknowledge the holy in all music played to glorify God. The only cautions are avoiding raucous tunes or renditions and being alert to tune names. If you print the titles to all music in your bulletin, be aware that some tune names may sound as if the music is unsuitable for a worship environment. If you must print the title for something like *Neil Gow's Lament upon the Death of his Second Wife* or *Whiskey in the Jar*, a little research almost always yields an alternate tune name if one is desired.

Celtic music technically is that from Celtic lands, i.e. Ireland, Scotland, Wales, Cape Breton, Brittany, and the Isle of Man. However, many tunes from England, early America, and other lands can sound Celtic and fit in right alongside other Celtic tunes when played on the right mix of instruments.

You can add singing as appropriate to the abilities of your congregation and of your musicians. We have two or three pieces of service music for each service. We also have compiled some hymns – many with contemporary words set to traditional tunes. Some traditional American tunes (such as *Beach Spring*) and some traditional Celtic tunes (such as *Slane* and *Kingsfold*) often have several sets of texts from which to choose. Be sure you follow copyright and licensing protocols when you reprint music in your church bulletin.

Enhancing worship with symbolic actions or accessories

The use of symbolic actions and accessories during the worship service serves to tie the words of the liturgy to the physical world in a concrete way that honors the physical and makes our actions sacred. These can take almost any form your congregation finds meaningful, but several are recommended here that have been found to be both meaningful and practical.

The church year opens with Advent when our liturgical theme is the element of sound. A chime (handbell, hand chime or singing bowl) can be sounded at designated moments during the service. Sounding the chimes six or eight times during the course of the service seems a good number; too many can be disruptive, but there should be enough that the additional sound is noticed. A rubric or announcement can explain that a chime will sound intermittently to call us into holy listening. The Christmas season when we celebrate the Nativity comes and goes so quickly; we have omitted any special symbolic actions.

Epiphany (along with the season that follows it) is the time when we mark the spreading of the light of Christ to the world, so lighting a candle is an appropriate action during this season. Many parishes use lots of candles for a Celtic service all the time, but saving the use of *lots* of lights for the season of light makes it more special. There can be a tray of votive candles in the back of the church or up near the communion rail or on a side aisle. Any arrangement that works safely for your space and time configuration is acceptable. Be sure that you consider fire safety when planning the use of candles. Other candles can be added to the worship space as well.

During Lent – the penitential season when we prepare for Easter – the use of a rock cairn can be meaningful. Small rocks can be available as congregants enter; they are encouraged to take a rock and then to place it on the cairn (possibly at the foot of the altar) as they come forward for communion. The rock can symbolize the burdens that we offer up to God – burdens we are especially aware of during Lent – or prayers or intentions that we bring before God. The sense of community can be felt as well, since we place our rock on the communal pile that is the cairn.

In Easter season, an abundance of plant and/or flower material can bring the joy of creation inside the church building. Again some churches use as much greenery as possible for all Celtic services. Of course, an outdoor chapel is also a fabulous place to celebrate God's creation, but few churches are blessed with such facilities. Potted plants – including large ones like ficus trees – can be effective. Any way that you can increase the amount of flower and foliage visible to the congregation is great for this season.

Following Easter, Pentecost is the feast day that marks the coming of the Holy Spirit among the disciples. Since this event was accompanied by a rushing wind as well as flames, both fire and wind are appropriate themes for the season after Pentecost, the longest of the church year. For symbolic actions, lighting candles can once again be used to symbolize the fire of the Holy Spirit.

A liturgy is also included for All Saints' Sunday (the first Sunday in November) or for any service including baptism. As the theme is water, a small fountain is ideal for this occasion, although it may be difficult to arrange in a sanctuary. If there is baptism, the font should be clearly visible to the people, and the water should be loudly and joyfully splashed as much as possible!

A final note about accessories: it is in keeping with the nature of the Celtic service to seek more rustic altar accessories than the standard brass candlesticks. Ceramic, wrought iron, or wood can be effective materials for chalice, paten, candle holders, offering plate, etc.

Do I need permission to use these liturgies?

Anyone may use the liturgies in this book for worship purposes. In the Episcopal Church, the liturgies that are officially allowed for use during each Sunday's primary worship service must be those sanctioned by the Church. In our parish we offer the Celtic service at 5 pm on Sundays; hence it is not our primary service. Therefore, we are able to exercise some liturgical flexibility. Alternatively, exceptions to this rule can be made if special permission is obtained from the appropriate bishop. If you are using this liturgy in an Episcopal church or another church which regulates the liturgies permitted, it is advisable that you check the regulations or expectations in your diocese and secure the appropriate permission.

The Structure of the Liturgy

The service begins with a few **opening words**, which offer a call to worship and introduce the theme.

There follows the **lighting of the three lights**. This appears in a number of Celtic liturgies and sets the tone nicely. It is generally easier for a server or acolyte to light the candles, freeing the priest to attend to the accompanying words. The candles should be large and visible to as much of the congregation as possible. To keep the congregation engaged, the words can be said responsively.

The **opening prayer** is included next. A standard one is the Collect for Purity from *The Book of Common Prayer*, which here has been paraphrased.

A **hymn of praise** now follows; in a standard service from *The Book of Common Prayer*, this would be the Gloria. We offer praise to God not only for the standard blessings, but especially for the natural world. We do not sing this "hymn," but you could use one set to music if you have one.

The **readings and sermon** now follow. It is nice to include an "Alleluia" such as the "Celtic Alleluia" before the Gospel if you have music. We also use poetry in place of the psalm or one of the readings. There are a lot of good Celtic or Celtic-style poems available. Again, poetry based on the themes can be most effective.

After the sermon, it is time for the **creed** or **affirmation of faith.** Although the Celtic Church did not have a well-established, separate creed (they probably said the Nicene Creed), you may choose to say a different creed in such an otherwise contemporary service. The adaptation of

Tirechan's creed offers a good alternative – it is from an ancient Celtic source, but has been paraphrased with contemporary language.

There are several versions of the **prayers of the people**, some of which are nicely tailored to the seasonal theme. You can also write your own intercessions, and of course, be sure to make time for others to add their personal prayers – aloud if possible.

Celtic liturgies often do not include a **confession**. The ancient Celtic focus which we like to highlight was that of celebrating what was going right, not in groveling about what had gone wrong. However, as Christian liturgies generally include a confession, there are some offered. The confession is usually suppressed during the seasons of Christmas and Easter; during Lent it can be moved to the beginning of the service as it is in *The Book of Common Prayer*'s Penitential Order.

The words of the **peace** were taken from *The New Women Included* by the St. Hilda Community – a community in England which spent many years advocating for the ordination of women in England. Their liturgical materials were innovative as were their voices of advocacy.

Almost all the **Eucharistic prayers** are adapted from J. Philip Newell's prayers in *An Earthful of Glory*. This is one of the few books that has Celtic-style communion liturgies, in addition to other prayers. The one used in Lent, however, is taken from Newell's *A Celtic Mass for Peace*. (I obtained a copy of this when with Philip on Iona in 2005; in addition, Redeemer used this liturgy when Philip came to our parish in 2007.) This mass has been set to music by Sam Guarnaccia, and although it is not Celtic or Celtic-style music, it is quite lovely and haunting.

The **Sanctus** remains a part of every Eucharistic prayer, and the words are the same as in *The Book of Common Prayer*. This is intended so that any standard musical setting will work if you will be singing it. *Land of Rest* is a good one. The Eucharistic prayer ends with the **breaking of the bread.**

The **closing prayers** give us the opportunity to thank God for the holy meal and for the love which it represents. Usually the liturgical theme is woven back into this prayer. Following that is the **lights-out prayer** – when we extinguish the three lights. The special nature of these last two prayers is almost magical – a magic that you may not want to break with mundane parish announcements; it is recommended that announcements are taken care of earlier in the service. We end with a **blessing and dismissal.**

A variety of these elements combine to create each liturgy in this book. The services are formatted according to the custom at the Church of the Redeemer. You may use these liturgies as printed or create your own. To create your own liturgy, you can mix and match these elements. Not all elements are necessary. For example, we generally omit the three lights in Lent, and some omit the confession in Easter and Christmas seasons. The liturgies as compiled here are structured with a Celtic theological emphasis and the seasonal focus in mind, but can be rearranged to fit your parish's needs and customs.

**A Celebration of the Holy Eucharist
in the Celtic Tradition
for the Season of Advent:
Waiting and Listening for God**

Opening Words
Celebrant
   The God of love is with us.
People
   The Spirit of love is in us.
Celebrant
   Blessed be the one God,
   whose prophets foretold the coming of the Light;
People
   And blessed be the Son, whose coming we await.

The Lighting of the Three Lights
Celebrant
   We will light a light in the name of the Maker –
People
   God who spoke in the silence and gave the gift of sound.
Celebrant
   We will light a light in the name of Christ –
People
   Jesus, whose human ears heard
   the sounds of his Father's creation.
Celebrant
   We will light a light in the name of the Spirit –
People
   The Holy One who speaks to us with a still, small voice.

Opening Prayer
Celebrant
   The Lord be with you.

People

And also with you.

Celebrant

Let us pray.

Almighty and eternal God, to you our hearts are open and our inmost desires known; we cannot hide our most intimate secrets from you. We ask you to be present at all times in our thoughts and our hearts and to purify them, so that we may love you with the love of the Spirit and praise your name with humility and joy; through Christ our Lord.

All

Amen.

A Hymn of Praise

Celebrant

Let us praise the Holy One in the words of Mary.

All

My soul proclaims the greatness of the Lord,
    my spirit rejoices in God my Savior;
    for he has looked with favor on his lowly servant.
From this day all generations will call me blessed:
    the Almighty has done great things for me,
    and holy is his Name.
He has mercy on those who fear him in every generation.
He has shown the strength of his arm,
    he has scattered the proud in their conceit.
He has cast down the mighty from their thrones,
    and has lifted up the lowly.
He has filled the hungry with good things,
    and the rich he has sent away empty.
He has come to the help of his servant Israel,
    for he has remembered his promise of mercy,
    the promise he made to our fathers,
    to Abraham and his children for ever.

A Prayer for the Day

Celebrant
  The Lord be with you.
People
  And also with you.
Celebrant
  Let us pray.
<Here is read a prayer or collect selected for the day.>

The First Reading

<After the reading, the people respond>
  Thanks be to God.

A Psalm or Poem

The Second Reading

<After the reading, the people respond>
  Thanks be to God.

<A hymn or anthem or "Alleluia" may be sung here.>

The Gospel

Deacon or Celebrant
  The Holy Gospel of our Lord Jesus Christ . . .
People
  Glory to you, Lord Christ.
<Here the Gospel is read, the people facing the reader.>
Deacon or Celebrant
  The Gospel of the Lord.
People
  Praise to you, Lord Christ.

The Sermon

An Affirmation of Faith

Celebrant

Let us join in affirming our faith in God.

All

We believe in God above us,
    maker and sustainer of all life,
    of sun and moon, of water and earth,
    of male and female.
We believe in God beside us, Jesus Christ,
    the Word made flesh,
    born of a woman, servant of the poor,
    tortured and nailed to a tree.
A man of sorrows, he died forsaken.
He descended into the earth to the place of death.
On the third day he rose from the tomb.
He ascended into heaven, to be everywhere present,
    and his kingdom will come on earth.
We believe in God within us,
    the Holy Spirit of pentecostal fire,
    life-giving breath of the Church,
    Spirit of healing and forgiveness,
    source of resurrection and of eternal life. Amen.

The Prayers of the People

Celebrant

With prayers for a world waiting in hope,
    let us turn to the Lord, and we shall be saved.

Intercessor

For the Church, still waiting for unity,
    still hoping for renewal.
May all the faithful be blessed by the sound of the Gospel
    proclaimed to the ends of the earth.

People

Come, Lord Jesus, hear our prayer.

Intercessor

For all nations, still waiting for peace,
    still hoping for an end to war,
    still searching for common ground.
May all peoples be blessed by the sound of
    understanding between clans and tribes,
    rulers and races.

People

Come, Lord Jesus, hear our prayer.

Intercessor

For those who have lost hope, still waiting for a job,
    still hoping for a cure,
    still searching for a place to call home.
May those without joy this season be blessed by the
    sound of God's promise for them fulfilled.

People

Come, Lord Jesus, hear our prayer.

Intercessor

For travelers and visitors, families and friends,
    still waiting for welcome,
    still hoping for reconciliation,
    still searching for a way to mend
    what has been broken.
May everyone we encounter this season be blessed
    by greetings of peace, compassion, and hospitality.

People

Come, Lord Jesus, hear our prayer.

Intercessor

For the sick and the dying and those who care for them,
    still waiting for results, still hoping for a miracle,
    still searching for courage and comfort,
    including those we now name,
    either silently or aloud.   *<Pause>*
May all the sick be blessed by the sound of God's healing
    word and the strength of our prayers.

People

Come, Lord Jesus, hear our prayer.

Intercessor

For the dead – loved ones whom we miss this season,
    forgotten ones who died alone,
        innocent ones caught in the crossfire of violence,
        including those we now name
        either silently or aloud.   *<Pause>*
May all who have died be blessed
    by the sound of God welcoming them home.

People

Come, Lord Jesus, hear our prayer.

Celebrant

You are near to us, Lord, as close to us
    as the child in the womb of her mother.
And yet we wait in expectant hope for your coming.
Attune our ears to hear your voice in all those we meet,
    and open our eyes to see
    your abiding presence in our world.
Hear our prayers and make us turn to you
    that we may leap for joy at the sound
    of your saving Word, Jesus, Emmanuel,
    God with us, for ever and ever.

People

Amen.

Confession and Forgiveness

Celebrant

As we await the coming of Jesus,
    so we often wait for others to forgive us.
Our sin separates us from God and from one another.
Let us forgive our brothers and sisters
    and confess our own sin together.

All

God of all people, as we await once again
the birth of your love in our hearts,
we confess that we have lost sight of that love.
In this busy season we turn away from pain and poverty,
we avoid the sick and the lonely,
and we ignore the outcast and the oppressed.
Have mercy on us and give us the strength
to truly welcome Christ into our hearts
and to live our lives according to your will.
We ask this in Jesus' name. Amen.

Celebrant

The Lord enrich us with grace,
and further us with heavenly blessing.
The Lord defend us in adversity and keep us from all evil.
The Lord receive our prayers
and graciously absolve us from our offenses.
In God's name we pray.

All

Amen.

Sharing the Peace

Celebrant

God makes peace within us

People

Let us claim it.

Celebrant

God makes peace between us.

People

Let us share it.

Announcements and Offertory

The Great Thanksgiving

Celebrant

The Lord be with you.

People

And also with you.

Celebrant

Lift up your hearts.

People

We lift them to the Lord.

Celebrant

Let us give thanks to the Lord our God.

People

It is right to give our thanks and praise.

Celebrant

All things are yours, O God of all creation,

People

And so we return our gifts of treasure to you.

Celebrant

Blessed are you, O God of creation, through whose goodness we have this bread to offer, which earth has given and human hands have made;

People

May it become for us the bread of life.

Celebrant

Blessed are you, O God of creation, through whose goodness we have this wine to offer, fruit of the vine and work of human hands;

People

May it become for us the cup of blessing.

Celebrant

Receive these gifts, dear God, and accept in them the sacrifice of ourselves.

People

In life and in death may we be an offering to you for ever.

Celebrant

We offer you praise and hearts lifted high, O God, who is Father of all life and of all sound. Though our days vanish like mist, and the sounds of the earth fade away in the distance, still your Spirit is within all life, and every human soul is born in your likeness. And so with the whole created order, with the stars that silently glisten with life's glory, with the wind that howls and the gentle breeze that whispers, with the trumpets of heaven's messengers and the echo of the saints, we join in the song of your unending greatness:

The Sanctus
All

Holy, holy, holy Lord, God of power and might.
　　Heaven and earth are full of your glory.
　　Hosanna in the highest!
Blessed is the One who comes in the name of the Lord!
　　Hosanna in the highest!

The Eucharistic Prayer
Celebrant

Blessed are you, O God, whose wisdom from above has inspired men and women through the ages to fulfill on earth your purposes – to hear the cry of the poor, to act with mercy, and to live together in gentleness and peace. We bless you for the coming of Christ, who in life and in death embodied the law of love. By his rising again, he has saved our souls from despair, and by the gift of the Holy Spirit, he has given us courage and hope to face the forces of evil and death that rage around and within us.

On the night he was betrayed, Jesus took bread, and having blessed it, he broke the bread, and gave it to his disciples, saying, "Take, eat, this is my body which is broken for you. Do this in remembrance of me." In the

same way he took wine, and having given thanks for it,
he shared it with his disciples, saying, "This cup is the
new covenant in my blood. Do this as often as you drink
it, in remembrance of me."

People

Remembering his eternal self-giving, we proclaim the
mystery of Christ among us. Made one with him, and one
with each other, we offer these gifts, and with them
ourselves, a single, holy living sacrifice.

Celebrant

O God, whose generosity is unbounded and who wills
that we should lack no good thing, bless this bread and
this wine with your Holy Spirit, that in receiving them
into ourselves we may be made whole again,
strengthened not merely to hear the truth, but to do it,
and be blessed in our doing; through Christ, by whom,
with whom, and in whom, in the unity of the Holy Spirit,
all glory and honor is yours, almighty God, world without
end.

All

Amen.

The Lord's Prayer

Celebrant

And now as our Savior Christ has taught us, we pray:

All

Our Father in heaven, hallowed be your Name,
  your kingdom come, your will be done,
    on earth as in heaven.
Give us today our daily bread.
Forgive us our sins
  as we forgive those who sin against us.
Save us from the time of trial, and deliver us from evil.
For the kingdom, the power,
  and the glory are yours, now and forever. Amen.

The Breaking of the Bread
Celebrant

    The Spirit we await is with us in this bread.

People

    The voice of the Holy One speaks to us in this cup.

The Sharing of a Holy Meal

The Closing Prayers
Celebrant

    Let us stand and join in thanking God for this holy meal.

All

    O God, we have heard your call to us,

        and we have responded by gathering in your name
        to await your voice.

    Help us to listen to your presence

        in silence and in sound – the voices of your people,
        the noises of your animals, the music of creation –
        that, reconnected with you and one another
        through this holy meal,
        we may hear the voice which calls us home to you,
        our Creator, Redeemer, and Sanctifier. Amen.

Celebrant

    Lord of all light, as we go forth into the world,

        we extinguish the lights that here represent
        the presence of the Holy in our midst,

People

    But we will carry the light in our hearts,

        and we pray that as we go about our work in the
        world, we will shine with the love of God. Amen.

The Blessing
Celebrant

    May the Wonderful Counselor guide you,

        the Mighty God protect you,

the Everlasting Father be with you,
and the Prince of Peace comfort you.
And the blessing of God, Father, Son and Holy Spirit,
be upon you now and ever more.

All
Amen.

The Dismissal

Celebrant
Let us go forth with joy to love and serve the Lord.

People
Thanks be to God!

A Celebration of the Holy Eucharist
in the Celtic Tradition
for the Season of the Nativity:
The Gift of Love at Christmastide

Opening Words
Celebrant
> The God of love is with us.

People
> The Spirit of love is in us.

Celebrant
> Blessed is the one God, who gave us the gift of Jesus.

People
> Blessed is the Christ Child, whose birth is the gift of love.

The Lighting of the Three Lights
Celebrant
> We will light a light in the name of the Maker –

People
> Who gives us the power of life.

Celebrant
> We will light a light in the name of Christ –

People
> Who gives us the power of love.

Celebrant
> We will light a light in the name of the Spirit –

People
> Who gives us the power of hope.

Opening Prayer
Celebrant
> The Lord be with you.

People
> And also with you.

Celebrant

Let us pray.

Lord God, who by the incarnation of Jesus cast away the darkness of the world; be near us as the dark approaches and dispel the gloom of night that we may see your light and that your brightness may shine through us to your glory; through Christ our Lord, who lives and reigns with you and the Holy Spirit, one God, world without end.

All

Amen.

A Hymn of Praise

Celebrant

God brings light and hope through the gift of Jesus.

Let us give glory and praise to God.

People

We give you praise for your child born among us, O God.

Glory, glory, glory!

Celebrant

A promised birth, conceived and awaited in love,

People

Heaven's son come among us, sent to redeem the earth.

Glory, glory, glory!

Celebrant

Stars of the open sky, sun that shines
and moon that glows.

People

All these that shine glimmer with gladness at this birth.

Glory, glory, glory!

Celebrant

The whole earth's radiance shines forth
to welcome the Savior.

People

For all your radiance, for all your love, we give you praise.

Glory, glory, glory!

Celebrant
   To God born to us and God born among us,
People
   To God born within us. Glory, glory, glory! Amen.

A Prayer for the Day
Celebrant
   The Lord be with you.
People
   And also with you.
Celebrant
   Let us pray.
<Here is read a prayer or collect selected for the day.>

The First Reading
<After the reading, the people respond>
   Thanks be to God.

A Psalm or Poem

The Second Reading
<After the reading, the people respond>
   Thanks be to God.

<A hymn or anthem or "Alleluia" may be sung here.>

The Gospel
Deacon or Celebrant
   The Holy Gospel of our Lord Jesus Christ . . .
People
   Glory to you, Lord Christ.
<Here the Gospel is read, the people facing the reader.>
Deacon or Celebrant
   The Gospel of the Lord.

Praise to you, Lord Christ.

The Sermon

An Affirmation of Faith
Celebrant
Let us affirm our faith in God.
All
We believe in God above us,
maker and sustainer of all life,
of sun and moon, of water and earth,
of male and female.
We believe in God beside us, Jesus Christ,
the Word made flesh,
born of a woman, servant of the poor,
tortured and nailed to a tree.
A man of sorrows, he died forsaken.
He descended into the earth to the place of death.
On the third day he rose from the tomb.
He ascended into heaven, to be everywhere present,
and his kingdom will come on earth.
We believe in God within us,
the Holy Spirit of pentecostal fire,
life-giving breath of the Church,
Spirit of healing and forgiveness,
source of resurrection and of eternal life. Amen.

The Prayers of the People
Celebrant
We pray now for the needs of the earth and all its people,
remembering that God fulfills our greatest need – the
need for love – in the gift of his Son. Let us pray.

Intercessor
   Christ, heralded by the angels,
      open our eyes to your presence.
People
   Graciously hear us, Lord.
Intercessor
   Christ, born of the blessed Virgin,
      teach us obedience to your Word.
People
   Graciously hear us, Lord.
Intercessor
   Christ, born in a stable,
      give hope to the homeless.
People
   Graciously hear us, Lord.
Intercessor
   Christ, visited by the shepherds,
      strengthen all who work on the land.
People
   Graciously hear us, Lord.
Intercessor
   Christ, adored by wise ones,
      guide all rulers and governments.
People
   Graciously hear us, Lord.
Intercessor
   Christ, exiled in Egypt,
      give comfort to all refugees.
People
   Graciously hear us, Lord.
Intercessor
   We now pray for our own needs and for those of others,
   either silently or aloud. *<Pause.>*

Celebrant

Gracious God, you have revealed your love by the coming of our Lord Jesus Christ into our world. Help us to welcome him with joy, and to make room for him in our lives and homes, that we may abide in him and he in us; through the same Christ our Lord, who lives and reigns with you, O God, and the Holy Spirit, now and for ever. Amen.

Sharing the Peace

Celebrant

God makes peace within us.

People

Let us claim it.

Celebrant

God makes peace between us.

People

Let us share it.

Announcements and Offertory

The Great Thanksgiving

Celebrant

The Lord be with you.

People

And also with you.

Celebrant

Lift up your hearts.

People

We lift them to the Lord.

Celebrant

Let us give thanks to the Lord our God.

People

It is right to give God thanks and praise.

Celebrant

All things are yours, O God of creation,

People

And so we return our gifts of treasure to you.

Celebrant

Blessed are you, O God of creation,
through whose goodness we have this bread to offer,
which earth has given and human hands have made;

People

May it become for us the bread of life.

Celebrant

Blessed are you, O God of creation, through whose
goodness we have this wine to offer, fruit of the vine and
work of human hands;

People

May it become for us the cup of blessing.

Celebrant

Receive these gifts, dear God, and accept in them the
sacrifice of our selves.

People

In life and in death may we be an offering to you for ever.

Celebrant

We offer you praise and hearts lifted high, O God, whose
light enlightens every human being, and whose love
offers to all hope for new life. And so with the whole
realm of nature around us, with earth, sea, and sky, with
the light of sun and stars, with angels of light, with saints
of heaven and of earth, we join in the song of your
unending greatness:

The Sanctus

All

Holy, holy, holy Lord, God of power and might.
Heaven and earth are full of your glory.
Hosanna in the highest!

Blessed is the One who comes in the name of the Lord!
Hosanna in the highest!

The Eucharistic Prayer
Celebrant

Holy in the heights of heaven, holy in the depths of earth,
O God, your glory knows no bounds, and your love is
without end. The Word that was in the beginning, and
through whom all things were made, you sent to dwell
among us, full of grace and truth, that believing in him
we may have springs of life within. We bless you that in
love for the world, your Son laid down his life and
overcame death's powers to be our hope of life
everlasting; that in love he poured out his Spirit to lead
us through encircling darkness into all truth; and that in
love he returned to the Source of Light to draw all the
earth to himself.

To the very end Jesus loved those whom he had been
given, and prayed that his love might be in them. On the
night he was betrayed, Jesus took bread, and having
blessed it, he broke the bread and gave it to his friends,
saying, "Take, eat, this is my body which is broken for
you. Do this for the remembrance of me." In the same
way he took wine and, having given thanks for it, poured
it out and gave the cup to them, saying, "Drink this, all of
you: This is my blood which is poured out for you.
Whenever you drink it, do this for the remembrance of
me."

All

Remembering his eternal self-giving, we proclaim the
mystery of Christ among us. Made one with him, and one
with each other, we offer these gifts and with them
ourselves, a single, holy living sacrifice.

Celebrant

Hear us now, O Christ, and breathe your Spirit upon us, and upon this bread and this wine, that they may be heaven's food and drink for us, for you are the living bread that comes down from heaven to give life to the world; you are the true vine without whom we can do nothing. We pray in the name of Christ by whom, with whom, and in whom, in the unity of the Holy Spirit, all glory and honor is yours, almighty God, world without end.

All

Amen.

The Lord's Prayer

Celebrant

As our Savior Christ has taught us, we now pray:

All

Our Father in heaven, hallowed be your Name,
    your kingdom come, your will be done,
        on earth as in heaven.
Give us today our daily bread.
Forgive us our sins
    as we forgive those who sin against us.
Save us from the time of trial, and deliver us from evil.
For the kingdom, the power,
    and the glory are yours, now and forever. Amen.

The Breaking of the Bread

Celebrant

Bread of life, nourish our souls.

People

Light of the world, shine in our hearts.

The Sharing of a Holy Meal

The Closing Prayers
Celebrant

Let us thank God for this holy meal.

All

O God, in love you have called us to be your people,
    and in love we have shared this bread and this wine.
May the Spirit of your son Jesus, which is love,
    be born in us this Christmas.
May that Spirit drive away fear and anxiety
    and bring us life and hope;
    in the name of God,
    Creator, Redeemer, and Sanctifier. Amen.

Celebrant

Lord of all light, as we go forth into the world,
    we extinguish the lights that here represent
    the presence of the Holy in our midst,

People

But we will carry the light in our hearts,
    and we pray that as we go about
    our work in the world,
    we will shine with the love of God. Amen.

The Blessing
Celebrant

May the Wonderful Counselor guide you,
    the Mighty God protect you;
    the Everlasting Father be with you,
    and the Prince of Peace comfort you,
And the blessing of God, Father, Son and Holy Spirit,
    be with you and remain with you always.

All

Amen.

The Dismissal

Celebrant
Let us go forth in the world
with the love of Christ in our hearts.

People
Thanks be to God!

**A Celebration of the Holy Eucharist
in the Celtic Tradition for
the Season of Epiphany:
Sharing the Light of Christ**

Opening Words

Celebrant
   The God of love is with us.
People
   The Spirit of love is in us.
Celebrant
   Risen Lord, light of all peoples, come stand among us.
People
   Scatter the darkness before us
   that we may walk as children of light.

The Lighting of the Three Lights
Celebrant
   We will light a light in the name of the Maker –
People
   God who said, "Let there be light!"
Celebrant
   We will light a light in the name of Christ –
People
   Jesus whose birth was announced
   by the shining of a star.
Celebrant
   We will light a light in the name of the Spirit –
People
   The Holy One whose love enlightens our hearts.

Opening Prayer
Celebrant
   The Lord of light be with you.

People

And also with you.

Celebrant

Let us pray.

Lord God, who by the incarnation of Jesus cast away the darkness of the world; be near us as the dark approaches and dispel the gloom of night that we may see your light and that your brightness may shine through us to your glory; through Jesus Christ our Lord, who lives and reigns with you and the Holy Spirit, one God, world without end.

All

Amen.

A Hymn of Praise

Celebrant

God brings light to our darkened lives.

Let us praise the God of light!

O Christ, be our light;

People

O Lord, shine in the darkness and guide us on our path.

Celebrant

O Christ, be our shield;

People

O Lord, enfold us in your love and protect us in your care.

Celebrant

O Christ, surround us;

People

O Lord, be under us and be over us.

Celebrant

O Christ, embrace us;

People

O Lord, be beside us, on left and on right.

Celebrant

O Christ, lead and support us;

People
   O Lord, be before us and be behind us.
Celebrant
   O Christ, encompass us;
People
   O Lord, be within us and all around us.
Celebrant
   O Christ, be our light;
People
   O Lord, illumine and guide us on our way. Amen.

A Prayer for the Day
Celebrant
   The Lord be with you.
People
   And also with you.
Celebrant
   Let us pray.
<Here is read a prayer or collect selected for the day.>

The First Reading
<After the reading, the people respond>
   Thanks be to God.

A Psalm or Poem

<For a reading or the psalm, the following may be used.>

A Canticle of Light
   Arise, shine, for your light has come,
      and the glory of the Lord has dawned upon you.
   For behold, darkness covers the land;
      deep gloom enshrouds the peoples.
   But over you the Lord will rise,
      and his glory will appear upon you.

Nations will stream to your light,
    and kings to the brightness of your dawning.
Your gates will always be open;
    by day or night they will never be shut.
They will call you, The City of the Lord,
    The Zion of the Holy One of Israel.
Violence will no more be heard in your land,
    ruin or destruction within your borders.
You will call your walls, Salvation,
    and all your portals, Praise.
The sun will no more be your light by day;
    by night you will not need
    the brightness of the moon.
The Lord will be your everlasting light,
    and your God will be your glory.

The Second Reading
<After the reading, the people respond>
    Thanks be to God.

<A hymn or anthem or "Alleluia" may be sung here.>

The Gospel
Deacon or Celebrant
    The Holy Gospel of our Lord Jesus Christ . . .
People
    Glory to you, Lord Christ.
<Here the Gospel is read, the people facing the reader.>
Deacon or Celebrant
    The Gospel of the Lord.
People
    Praise to you, Lord Christ.

The Sermon

An Affirmation of Faith

Celebrant

Let us affirm our faith in God.

All

We believe in God above us,
   maker and sustainer of all life,
   of sun and moon, of water and earth,
   of male and female.
We believe in God beside us, Jesus Christ,
   the Word made flesh,
   born of a woman, servant of the poor,
   tortured and nailed to a tree.
A man of sorrows, he died forsaken.
He descended into the earth to the place of death.
On the third day he rose from the tomb.
He ascended into heaven, to be everywhere present,
   and his kingdom will come on earth.
We believe in God within us,
   the Holy Spirit of pentecostal fire,
   life-giving breath of the Church,
   Spirit of healing and forgiveness,
   source of resurrection and of eternal life. Amen.

The Prayers of the People

Celebrant

We pray now for the needs of all people throughout the
world, remembering that God brings light to any
darkness. Let us pray.

Intercessor

Gracious God, empower the Church throughout the
world in its life and witness. Break down the barriers that
divide, so that united in your truth and love, the Church
may confess your name, share one baptism, sit at one
table, and serve you with one accord.

People

Light of the world, be known to us.

Intercessor

Guide the rulers of the nations. Move them to set aside their fear, greed and vain ambition, and to strive for justice and peace, so that all your children may be free.

People

Light of the world, be known to us.

Intercessor

Hear the cries of those who are hungry, homeless, and suffering, those near and those far. Give those of us who consume most of the earth's resources the will to reorder our lives, so that all may have their rightful share of food, care, shelter, and fullness of life.

People

Light of the world, be known to us.

Intercessor

Look with compassion on all who suffer illness and distress, especially those we now name. *<Pause>* Support them with your love and lead us to be healers for all we encounter, in the name of Christ.

People

Light of the world, be known to us.

Intercessor

With thanksgiving, we remember those who have died, saints who bore witness to your light, especially those we now name. *<Pause>* Allow us to persevere in faith, mercy, and love, and at the end of our lives to behold your glory.

People

Light of the world, be known to us.

Celebrant

O God, in your loving purpose, answer our prayers for your creation. By your grace, grant us the will and the

wisdom to make this world new, and all for the sake of
Jesus Christ our Savior.

All
Amen.

Confession and Forgiveness

Celebrant
We gather together in search of wholeness, but our
brokenness separates us from God and from one
another. Let us confess our sin against God and our
neighbor.

All
God of glory, you sent Jesus among us
    as the light of the world,
    to reveal your love for all people.
We confess that our sin and pride
    hide the brightness of your light.
We turn away from the poor, we ignore cries for justice,
    and we do not strive for peace.
In your mercy, cleanse us of our sin,
    and baptize us once again with your Spirit, that,
    forgiven and renewed,
    we may show forth your glory
    shining in the face of Jesus Christ. Amen.

Celebrant
Almighty God, who forgives all who truly repent,
    have mercy on you and set you free from sin,
    strengthen you in goodness,
    and keep you in eternal life;
    through Jesus Christ our Lord.

All
Amen.

Sharing the Peace
Celebrant
  God makes peace within us.
People
  Let us claim it.
Celebrant
  God makes peace between us.
People
  Let us share it.

Announcements and Offertory

The Great Thanksgiving
Celebrant
  The Lord be with you.
People
  And also with you.
Celebrant
  Lift up your hearts.
People
  We lift them to the Lord.
Celebrant
  Let us give thanks to the Lord our God.
People
  It is right to give God thanks and praise.
Celebrant
  All things are yours, O God of creation,
People
  And so we return our gifts of treasure to you.
Celebrant
  Blessed are you, O God of creation, through whose
  goodness we have this bread to offer, which earth has
  given and human hands have made;
People
  May it become for us the bread of life.

Celebrant

Blessed are you, O God of creation, through whose goodness we have this wine to offer, fruit of the vine and work of human hands;

People

May it become for us the cup of blessing.

Celebrant

Receive these gifts, dear God, and accept in them the sacrifice of our selves.

People

In life and in death may we be an offering to you for ever.

Celebrant

We offer you praise and hearts lifted high, O God, whose light enlightens every human being, and whose love offers to all hope for new life. And so with the whole realm of nature around us, with earth, sea, and sky, with the light of sun and stars, with angels of light, with saints of heaven and of earth, we join in the song of your unending greatness:

The Sanctus

All

Holy, holy, holy Lord; God of power and might.
    Heaven and earth are filled with your glory.
    Hosanna in the highest!
Blessed is the One who comes in the name of the Lord.
    Hosanna in the highest!

The Eucharistic Prayer

Celebrant

Holy in the heights of heaven, holy in the depths of earth, O God, your glory knows no bounds, and your love is without end. The Word that was in the beginning, and through whom all things were made, you sent to dwell among us, full of grace and truth, that believing in him we may have springs of life within. We bless you that in love for the world, your Son laid down his life and overcame death's powers to be our hope of life everlasting; that in love he poured out his Spirit to lead us through encircling darkness into all truth; and that in love he returned to the Source of Light to draw all the earth to himself.

To the very end Jesus loved those whom he had been given, and prayed that his love might be in them. On the night he was betrayed, Jesus took bread, and having blessed it, he broke the bread and gave it to his friends, saying, "Take, eat, this is my body which is broken for you. Do this for the remembrance of me." In the same way he took wine and, having given thanks for it, poured it out and gave the cup to them, saying, "Drink this, all of you: This is my blood which is poured out for you. Whenever you drink it, do this for the remembrance of me."

All

Remembering his eternal self-giving, we proclaim the mystery of Christ among us. Made one with him, and one with each other, we offer these gifts and with them ourselves, a single, holy living sacrifice.

Celebrant

Hear us now, O Christ, and breathe your Spirit upon us, and upon this bread and this wine, that they may be heaven's food and drink for us, for you are the living bread that comes down from heaven to give life to the world; you are the true vine without whom we can do nothing. We ask these things in the name of Jesus, by whom, with whom, and in whom, in the unity of the Holy Spirit, all glory and honor is yours, almighty God, world without end.

All

Amen.

The Lord's Prayer
Celebrant
As our Savior Christ has taught us, we now pray:
All
Our Father in heaven, hallowed be your Name,
your kingdom come, your will be done,
on earth as in heaven.
Give us today our daily bread.
Forgive us our sins
as we forgive those who sin against us.
Save us from the time of trial, and deliver us from evil.
For the kingdom, the power,
and the glory are yours, now and forever. Amen.

The Breaking of the Bread
Celebrant
Bread of life, nourish our souls.
People
Light of the world, shine in our hearts.

The Sharing of a Holy Meal

The Closing Prayers
All
O God, in love you have called us to be your people,
and in love we have shared this bread and wine.
May the flame of your love be rekindled in our hearts
by this holy meal and may its light guide us
on our journey and lead us home to you;
in the name of God, Creator, Redeemer,
and Sanctifier. Amen.
Celebrant
Lord of all light, as we go forth into the world,
we extinguish the lights that here represent
the presence of the Holy in our midst,

People
But we will carry the light in our hearts,
and we pray that as we go about
our work in the world,
we will shine with the love of God. Amen.

The Blessing
Celebrant
May the light of Christ be in our hearts,
the small light that glows like a great fire,
the warm light that feels like a great love,
the bright light that leads us on our way.
And may Christ's love so fill us
that we may be lights to the world.
And the blessing of God, Father, Son and Holy Spirit,
be with you and remain with you always.
All
Amen.

The Dismissal
Deacon
Let us go forth into the world to share the light of Christ.
People
Thanks be to God!

**A Celebration of the Holy Eucharist
in the Celtic Tradition
for the Season of Lent:
Peace and Penitence in Preparation for Easter**

Opening Words

Celebrant
    The God of peace is with us.
People
    The Spirit of peace is in us.
Celebrant
    Come, Lord Christ, come into our hearts.
People
    Come, Lord Christ, and bring us your peace.

The Lighting of the Three Lights
Celebrant
    We will light a light in the name of the Maker –
People
    The God of wisdom and the Author of all peace.
Celebrant
    We will light a light in the name of Christ –
People
    Jesus whose life modeled radical peace.
Celebrant
    We will light a light in the name of the Spirit –
People
    The Holy One who brings us peace and comfort.

Opening Prayer
Celebrant
    The Lord of peace be with you.
People
    And also with you.

Celebrant

Let us pray.

God of all peace, whose Spirit fills our hearts, be with us as we seek to share your peace that surpasses human understanding, that those whom we encounter on this earthly journey may see in our lives the reflection of your love; in the name of Christ.

All

Amen.

A Penitential Litany

Celebrant

Bless the Lord who forgives all our sins;

People

His mercy endures for ever.

Celebrant

Christ who died for our sins,
forgive the penitent.

People

Lord, have mercy.

Celebrant

Christ who shared our griefs,
comfort the sorrowing.

People

Lord, have mercy.

Celebrant

Christ who thirsted on the cross,
bring relief to the hungry.

People

Lord, have mercy.

Celebrant

Christ forsaken by all,
be with the lonely and the sad.

People

Christ, have mercy.

Celebrant
   Christ mocked and scorned,
      support the outcasts and rejected.
People
   Christ, have mercy.
Celebrant
   Christ who suffered great pain,
      be a strength to the weak.
People
   Christ, have mercy.
Celebrant
   Christ who died for us all,
      grant us your salvation.
People
   Lord, have mercy.
Celebrant
   Christ crucified, done to death, and buried,
      give us hope.
People
   Lord, have mercy.
Celebrant
   Christ who descended into hell,
      raise us to glory.
People
   Lord, have mercy.
Celebrant
   Bless the Lord who forgives all our sins;
People
   His mercy endures for ever.

Confession and Forgiveness
Celebrant
   We seek his mercy as we seek wholeness.
   Our brokenness separates us from God
      and from each other.

Let us confess our sins together.

All

God of mercy, you sent Jesus Christ to seek and save the lost. We confess that we have strayed from you and turned aside from your ways. We have followed our pride, failed in love, neglected justice and ignored truth. Have mercy, O God, and forgive our sin. Return us to the path of righteousness through Jesus Christ our Savior. Amen.

Celebrant

May the forgiveness of God, the love of Christ, and the peace of the Holy Spirit be in our hearts and guide our lives this day and always.

All

Amen.

A Prayer for the Day

Celebrant

The Lord be with you.

People

And also with you.

Celebrant

Let us pray.

<Here is read a prayer or collect selected for the day.>

The First Reading

<After the reading, the people respond>

Thanks be to God.

A Psalm or Poem

The Second Reading

<After the reading, the people respond>

Thanks be to God.

<A hymn or anthem or "Alleluia" may be sung here.>

The Gospel
Deacon or Celebrant
>The Holy Gospel of our Lord Jesus Christ . . .

People
>Glory to you, Lord Christ.

<Here the Gospel is read, the people facing the reader.>
Deacon or Celebrant
>The Gospel of the Lord.

People
>Praise to you, Lord Christ.

The Sermon

An Affirmation of Faith
Celebrant
>Let us join in affirming our faith in God.

All
>Our God is the God of all humanity,
>>of heaven and earth, of the seas and the rivers,
>>of the sun and the moon, and all the stars,
>
>God of the highest mountains and of the lowest valleys,
>>over heaven, in heaven, and under heaven.
>
>God is present in all things in heaven and earth and seas,
>>inspires all things, brings life to all things,
>>is over all things and supports all things.
>
>God makes the light of the sun to shine,
>>and surrounds the moon and stars,
>>brings water to the deserts
>>and places dry islands in the sea.
>
>God's Son lives as God lives, eternal and holy.
>The Holy Spirit breathes in the Father and the Son,
>>and the Holy Spirit lives in God the Christ.
>
>And God is forever. Amen.

The Prayers of the People

Celebrant

We pray now for the needs of all people throughout the world, remembering that God offers comfort and peace to all creatures.

Intercessor

We bless you and thank you, O God, for you have filled creation with the glory of life that glows.

People

We give thanks to you, O Lord.

Intercessor

We bless you for the light of the sun and the moon and the stars, for the cleansing goodness of the waters.

People

We give thanks to you, O Lord.

Intercessor

We bless you for the goodness that grows from the earth, which nourishes us and brings us life.

People

We give thanks to you, O Lord.

Intercessor

In remembering with thanks the times and places of plenty and well-being in our lives, we stand also in prayer with all who are denied these things, and we ask that all people not be forsaken in time of trouble.

People

Do not forsake us, O Lord.

Intercessor

Let the cry of the poor be heard, O God, in heaven and on earth; let the hungry be fed and the oppressed be set free.

People

Do not forsake us, O Lord.

Intercessor

Let those in our community who are sick or suffering

know healing in body and soul.
<Additional prayers may be added.>
    O God of all peace,
People
    Do not forsake us, O Lord.
Intercessor
    Welcome those who have died into the arms of your
    love, and comfort those who mourn them.
<Additional prayers may be added.>
    O God of all hope,
People
    Do not forsake us, O Lord.
Intercessor
    Let nations at war cease their strife, neighbors in conflict
    stop their arguments, and loved ones find peace at
    home.
People
    Do not forsake us, O Lord, but grant us your peace.
Celebrant
    Look, Lord, on your children, who love your name and
    need your care and your comfort. Let our hands bear
    your love to the world that all may know your peace. In
    Jesus' name we pray.
All
    Amen.

Sharing the Peace

Celebrant
    God makes peace within us.
People
    Let us claim it.
Celebrant
    God makes peace between us.
People
    Let us share it.

Announcements and Offertory

The Great Thanksgiving
Celebrant
   The Lord be with you.
People
   And also with you.
Celebrant
   Lift up your hearts.
People
   We lift them to the Lord.
Celebrant
   Let us give thanks to the Lord our God.
People
   It is right to give God thanks and praise.
Celebrant
   All things are yours, O God of creation,
People
   And so we return our gifts of treasure to you.
Celebrant
   Blessed are you, O God of creation, through whose
   goodness we have this bread to offer, which earth has
   given and human hands have made;
People
   May it become for us the bread of life.
Celebrant
   Blessed are you, O God of creation, through whose
   goodness we have this wine to offer, fruit of the vine and
   work of human hands;
People
   May it become for us the cup of blessing.
Celebrant
   Receive these gifts, dear God, and accept in them the
   sacrifice of our selves.

People

In life and in death may we be an offering to you for ever.

Celebrant

Great Creator Spirit, from whom all life comes forth, here we gather again with bread and with wine, seeking your presence, and your peace, longing once more to be nourished.

People

We hunger for wholeness in our lives, for unity on earth and for peace among the nations. And we know that only in your love can such peace and unity be found.

Celebrant

So with all that we are and all that we can give, we join with all of creation as we sing your praises:

The Sanctus

All

Holy, holy, holy Lord; God of power and might.
    Heaven and earth are filled with your glory.
    Hosanna in the highest!
Blessed is the One who comes in the name of the Lord.
    Hosanna in the highest!

The Eucharistic Prayer

Celebrant

Blessed is your creation, O Lord, for all the earth reflects your glory. Blessed is the fruit of the earth, which sustains us in this earthly life. And blessed is your Son Jesus, who came to heal and bring wholeness by the forgiveness of sins. In life and in death, he revealed your glory; in life and in death he awakens in us the hope that all powers of evil will fall and that your love will reign.

On the night before he suffered, Jesus took bread and, lifting it up and giving thanks to you, he blessed it, broke it and gave it to his friends, saying: "Take and eat this, for this is my body which is given for you." Then he took the cup, blessed the wine and gave it to them, saying: "Take and drink this, for this cup is my blood, which shall be shed for the forgiveness of all. Whenever you do these things, you shall remember me."

And so, Lord, in memory of Jesus, we your children offer to you these gifts. We call now on your Holy Spirit to bless them – the holy bread of life and the cup of eternal blessing – and to make them be for us the food of heaven.

People

Accept with them the sacrifice of our hearts that all who share in this bread and this cup may be blessed in your love and that through this love, we may be instruments of your peace. We pray this in the name of Jesus, your Son. Amen.

The Lord's Prayer
Celebrant

As our Savior Christ has taught us, we now pray:

All

Our Father in heaven, hallowed be your Name,
    your kingdom come, your will be done,
    on earth as in heaven.
Give us today our daily bread.
Forgive us our sins
    as we forgive those who sin against us.
Save us from the time of trial, and deliver us from evil.
For the kingdom, the power,
    and the glory are yours, now and forever. Amen.

The Breaking of the Bread
Celebrant

Broken bread, poured out wine,
    signs of Christ's self-giving;

People

    Broken bread, poured out wine,

        food for the human soul;

Celebrant

    Broken bread, poured out wine,

        sacrifice for the world's peace.

The Sharing of a Holy Meal

The Closing Prayers

Celebrant

    Let us pray.

All

    We give you thanks, O God, for calling us together and for sustaining us with this holy meal. This place is sacred, this time is sacred, and in the sacredness we have shared a mystery. May we in every place and time recognize the sacredness of life, and may we accept the mystery as we accept your love – with joyful faith and eternal hope; in Christ's name. Amen.

Celebrant

    Lord of all light, as we go forth into the world,

        we extinguish the lights that here represent

        the presence of the Holy in our midst,

People

    But we will carry the light in our hearts, and

        we pray that as we go about our work in the world,

        we will shine with the love of God. Amen.

The Blessing

Celebrant

    The circle of God keep us near.

    The circle of God give us cheer.

    The circle of God bless you from above.

    The circle of God enfold you in love.

And the blessing of God, Father, Son, and Holy Spirit,
be with you now and always.
All
Amen.

The Dismissal
Deacon or Celebrant
Let us go forth in the name of Christ.
People
Thanks be to God.

**A Celebration of the Holy Eucharist
in the Celtic Tradition
for the Season of Easter:
A Celebration of New Life**

Opening Words
Celebrant
Alleluia! Christ is risen.
People
The Lord is risen indeed. Alleluia!
Celebrant
Christ is alive in our hearts.
People
The God who is love dwells in us. Alleluia!

The Lighting of the Three Lights
Celebrant
We will light a light in the name of the Maker –
People
God the Creator of all life.
Celebrant
We will light a light in the name of Christ –
People
Jesus who offers us newness of life.
Celebrant
We will light a light in the name of the Spirit –
People
The Holy One whose presence sanctifies all creation.

Opening Prayer
Celebrant
The Lord of creation be with you.
People
And also with you.

Celebrant

Let us pray.

O God, you made the universe with all its marvelous
order, its atoms, worlds, and galaxies, and the infinite
complexity of living creatures: Grant that, as we probe
the mysteries of your creation, we may come to know
you more truly, and more fully understand the purpose
to which we are called; in the name of Christ our Lord.

All

Amen.

A Hymn of Praise

Celebrant

Let us praise the Holy One, the Creator,
   the Maker of all, the God of creation!
In the beginning God created the heavens and the earth.
And God said, "Let there be light!"

People

Let the light and the darkness bless you, O Lord,
   for you are the God of all creation.

Celebrant

The winds of new beginnings stirred,
   and the deep and everlasting waters flowed.

People

Let the winds and the waters bless you, O Lord,
   for you are the God of all creation.

Celebrant

God created the earth and the earth grew green,
   green with trees and fields and valleys.

People

Let the mountains and hills, the fields and the valleys
   all join to bless you, O Lord,
      for you are the God of all creation.

Celebrant

The great light ruled the day
and the gentle light ruled the night,
and they guided the seasons
and marked the days and years.

People

Let the sun and moon praise you, O Lord,
for you are the God of all creation.

Celebrant

The waters brought forth living creatures,
and the creatures filled the seas, roamed the earth,
and rose up to the sky.

People

Let the birds and the fish, the dogs and cats,
the cows and ostriches and giraffes all bless you,
O Lord, for you are the God of all creation.

Celebrant

God formed humans in his own likeness,
and so we carry your life within us, O Lord.

People

Let the people all praise you,
and let everything that can sing bless your Name,
O Lord, for you are the God of all creation. Amen.

A Prayer for the Day

Celebrant

The Lord be with you.

People

And also with you.

Celebrant

Let us pray.

<Here is read a prayer or collect selected for the day.>

The First Reading <After the reading, the people respond>

Thanks be to God.

A Psalm or Poem
The Second Reading
<After the reading, the people respond>
    Thanks be to God.

<A hymn or anthem or "Alleluia" may be sung here.>

The Gospel
Deacon or Celebrant
    The Holy Gospel of our Lord Jesus Christ . . .
People
    Glory to you, Lord Christ.
<Here the Gospel is read, the people facing the reader.>
Deacon or Celebrant
    The Gospel of the Lord.
People
    Praise to you, Lord Christ.

The Sermon

An Affirmation of Faith
Celebrant
    Let us join in affirming our faith in God.
All
    Our God is the God of all humanity,
        of heaven and earth, of the seas and the rivers,
        of the sun and the moon, and all the stars,
    God of the highest mountains and of the lowest valleys,
        over heaven, in heaven, and under heaven.
    God is present in all things in heaven and earth and seas,
        inspires all things, brings life to all things,
        is over all things and supports all things.
    God makes the light of the sun to shine,
        and surrounds the moon and stars,
        brings water to the deserts

and places dry islands in the sea.
God's Son lives as God lives, eternal and holy.
The Holy Spirit breathes in the Father and the Son,
    and the Holy Spirit lives in God the Christ.
And God is forever. Amen.

The Prayers of the People
Celebrant
    We pray now for the needs of all people throughout the
    world, remembering that God created all and loves all.
    Let us pray.
Intercessor
    Heavenly Father, we come before you with reverence
    and with faith that through our prayers your presence
    can bless. We pray for the Church that its mission may
    reach to the ends of the earth.
People
    May we be Christ to each other and light to the world.
Intercessor
    We pray for the world that its leaders may follow the
    path of justice and its peoples the way of peace.
People
    May we and all nations respect one another in freedom,
    truth, and love.
Intercessor
    We pray for our community that those who make
    decisions that affect the lives of others may be inspired
    by your wisdom.
People
    May we all act with integrity, respect, and courage that
    we may live together in harmony.
Intercessor
    We pray for those any need or trouble.
    <Particular intercessions are offered.>

God of hope, comfort and restore all who suffer in body, mind or spirit.

People

May they know the power of your healing love through human compassion.

Intercessor

We remember those who have died and those who mourn.   *<Particular intercessions are offered.>*

Father, into your hands we commend them.

People

Bring peace to those who mourn in their time of loss.

Intercessor

We pray for ourselves in this church community and for the ministries in which we serve God here.

<Particular intercessions are offered.>

Lord, you have called us to serve you.

All

Grant that we may walk in your presence with your truth in our minds, your strength in our souls and your love in our hearts, that we may share the light of your love with all, through Jesus Christ our Lord. Amen.

Sharing the Peace

Celebrant

God makes peace within us.

People

Let us claim it.

Celebrant

God makes peace between us.

People

Let us share it.

Announcements and Offertory

The Great Thanksgiving
Celebrant
  The Lord be with you.
People
  And also with you.
Celebrant
  Lift up your hearts.
People
  We lift them to the Lord.
Celebrant
  Let us give thanks to the Lord our God.
People
  It is right to give God thanks and praise.
Celebrant
  All things are yours, O God of creation,
People
  And so we return our gifts of treasure to you.
Celebrant
  Blessed are you, O God of creation, through whose
  goodness we have this bread to offer, which earth has
  given and human hands have made;
People
  May it become for us the bread of life.
Celebrant
  Blessed are you, O God of creation, through whose
  goodness we have this wine to offer, fruit of the vine and
  work of human hands;
People
  May it become for us the cup of blessing.
Celebrant
  Receive these gifts, dear God, and accept in them the
  sacrifice of our selves.
People
  In life and in death may we be an offering to you for ever.

Celebrant

We offer you praise and hearts lifted high, O God, by whose word the heavens were formed and the earth was brought forth from the waters. The reflection of your glory shines in each created thing, and though earth's flowering fades, you plant within us imperishable seeds for our salvation and call life out of death into the light that endures forever. And so with heaven and earth's host of light, with the sainted women and men of every nation, and with those who now live in the spirit as you are Spirit, we join in the song of your unending greatness:

The Sanctus
All

Holy, holy, holy Lord; God of power and might.
  Heaven and earth are filled with your glory.
  Hosanna in the highest!
Blessed is the One who comes in the name of the Lord.
  Hosanna in the highest!

The Eucharistic Prayer
Celebrant

Blessed are you, O God, for the great day of salvation prepared from the beginning of the world, when Christ, though rejected on earth, will be seen by all to be chosen and precious in your sight. We bless you for Christ who carried sin's destructive powers to the cross that we and all people might be set free. Through Christ you inspire the hope in us that earth's forces of darkness will be scattered, and angels of glory and principalities of light will bring a new heaven and a new earth.

Just as prophets long before Christ had spoken of the sufferings that would be his, so Jesus on the night when he was betrayed took bread, and having blessed it, he broke the bread, and gave it to his disciples, saying: "Take, eat; this is my body which is broken for you. Do this in remembrance of me." In the same way he took wine and, having given thanks for it, he poured it out, and gave the cup to his disciples, saying: "This cup is the new covenant in my blood. Do this, as often as you drink it, in remembrance of me."

People

Remembering his eternal self-giving, we proclaim the mystery of Christ among us. Made one with him and one with each other, we offer these gifts, and with them ourselves, a single, holy living sacrifice.

Celebrant

Bless us with your Holy Spirit, O God, and bless this bread and wine, that through them we may be made strong again with the strength that only you supply. May our inner selves be nourished that, in the outward things of life, we may follow the way of Christ and grow more and more into salvation; through Christ, by whom, with whom, and in whom, in the unity of the Holy Spirit, all glory and honor is yours, almighty God, world without end.

All

Amen.

The Lord's Prayer

Celebrant

As our Savior Christ has taught us, we now pray:

All

Our Father in heaven, hallowed be your Name,
   your kingdom come, your will be done,
      on earth as in heaven.
Give us today our daily bread.
Forgive us our sins
   as we forgive those who sin against us.

Save us from the time of trial, and deliver us from evil.
For the kingdom, the power,
and the glory are yours, now and forever. Amen.

The Breaking of the Bread
Celebrant
Gracious God, we come to your table;
People
Nourish us with the bread of life and the cup of heaven.

The Sharing of a Holy Meal

Closing Prayers
Celebrant
Let us pray.
All
O God, who has renewed the earth
by the gift of creation,
we thank you for opening our hearts
and making us new with this holy meal.
As we have shared this bread and wine,
may we also generously share our lives in love,
and as we seek you in your creation each day,
may we find the patience and vision
to see your love at work in all things
and the grace to let our lives reflect that love;
through Christ our Lord. Amen.
Celebrant
Lord of all light, as we go forth into the world,
we extinguish the lights that here represent
the presence of the Holy in our midst,
People
But we will carry the light in our hearts, and
we pray that as we go about our work in the world,
we will shine with the love of God. Amen.

The Blessing

Celebrant

The Lord of creation open your eyes
    to behold the beauty around you,
The Lord of light shine forth to guide you on your way,
    and the Lord of love enfold you in his arms,
    this day and every day.
And the blessing of God, Father, Son and Holy Spirit,
    be with you now and always.

All

Amen.

The Dismissal

Celebrant

Alleluia! Alleluia! Let us go forth in the name of Christ.

People

Thanks be to God. Alleluia! Alleluia!

**A Celebration of the Holy Eucharist
in the Celtic Tradition
for the Season after Pentecost:
The Fire of the Holy Spirit**

Opening Words
Celebrant
   The God of love is with us.
People
   The Spirit of love is in us.
Celebrant
   Blessed be the One whose Spirit burns in our hearts.
People
   May the Spirit set us afire with his love.

The Lighting of the Three Lights
Celebrant
   We will light a light in the name of the Maker –
People
   God who created fire.
Celebrant
   We will light a light in the name of Christ –
People
   Jesus whose love warms our hearts.
Celebrant
   We will light a light in the name of the Spirit –
People
   The Holy One, the fire of life.

Opening Prayer
Celebrant
   The Lord of love be with you.
People
   And also with you.

Celebrant

Let us pray.

Almighty and eternal God, to you our hearts are open, to you our inmost desires are known and we cannot hide our most intimate secrets from you. We ask you to be present at all times in our thoughts and our hearts and to purify them with your Holy Spirit, so that we may love you with the love of the Spirit and praise your name with humility and joy; through Christ our Lord.

All

Amen.

A Hymn of Praise

Celebrant

Let us praise the Holy One.

People

God sets our hearts afire with love.
Praise to the God of love!

Celebrant

As a fire warms the hands of those who venture near,
 so does the Spirit of our God warm the hearts
 of those who open their souls to his love.

People

Praise for the warmth!

Celebrant

As a fire surrounds all in its path,
 so does the Spirit of our God
 envelop our souls in grace.

People

Praise for the grace!

Celebrant

As a fire blazes with passionate intensity,
 so does the Spirit of our God set us on fire
 with a heavenly passion.

People
   Praise for the passion!
Celebrant
   Praise to the God of the hearth
      who invites us to draw near.
People
   Praise to the God of the flame,
      of the warmth, of the passion. Amen.

A Prayer for the Day
Celebrant
   The Lord be with you.
People
   And also with you.
Celebrant
   Let us pray.
<Here is read a prayer or collect selected for the day.>

The First Reading
<After the reading, the people respond>
   Thanks be to God.

A Psalm or Poem

The Second Reading
<After the reading, the people respond>
   Thanks be to God.

<A hymn or anthem or "Alleluia" may be sung here.>

The Gospel
Deacon or Celebrant
   The Holy Gospel of our Lord Jesus Christ . . .
People
   Glory to you, Lord Christ.

<Here the Gospel is read, the people facing the reader.>
Deacon or Celebrant
> The Gospel of the Lord.

People
> Praise to you, Lord Christ.

The Sermon

An Affirmation of Faith
Celebrant
> Let us join in affirming our faith in God.

All
> Our God is the God of all humanity,
>> of heaven and earth, of the seas and the rivers,
>> of the sun and the moon, and all the stars,
> God of the highest mountains and of the lowest valleys,
>> over heaven, in heaven, and under heaven.
> God is present in all things in heaven and earth and seas,
>> inspires all things, brings life to all things,
>> is over all things and supports all things.
> God makes the light of the sun to shine,
>> and surrounds the moon and stars,
>> brings water to the deserts
>> and places dry islands in the sea.
> God's Son lives as God lives, eternal and holy.
> The Holy Spirit breathes in the Father and the Son,
>> and the Holy Spirit lives in God the Christ.
> And God is forever. Amen.

The Prayers of the People
Celebrant
> We pray now for the Church, the world, and all those in
> need, remembering that God can be present to us and
> can transform our lives if we but draw near. Let us pray.

Intercessor

Gracious God, empower the Church throughout the world in its life and witness.
Break down the barriers that divide, so that united in your truth and love, the Church may confess your name, share one baptism, sit at one table, and serve you with one accord.

People

Light of the world, be known to us.

Intercessor

Guide the rulers of the nations. Move them to set aside their fear, greed and vain ambition, and to strive for justice and peace, so that all your children may be free.

People

Light of the world, be known to us.

Intercessor

Hear the cries of those who are hungry, homeless, and suffering, those near and those far.
Give those of us who consume most of the earth's resources the will to reorder our lives, so that all may have their rightful share of food, care, shelter, and fullness of life.

People

Light of the world, be known to us.

Intercessor

Look with compassion on all who suffer illness and distress, especially those we now name. *<Pause>*
Support them with your love and lead us to be healers for all we encounter, in the name of Christ.

People

Light of the world, be known to us.

Intercessor

With thanksgiving, we remember those who have died, saints who bore witness to your light, especially those we now name. *<Pause>*

Allow us to persevere in faith, mercy, and love, and at the end of our lives to behold your glory.

People

Light of the world, be known to us.

Celebrant

O God, in your loving purpose, answer our prayers for your creation. By your grace, grant us the will and the wisdom to make this world new, and all for the sake of Jesus Christ our Savior.

All

Amen.

Confession and Forgiveness

Deacon or Celebrant

We gather together in search of wholeness, but our sin separates us from God and from one another. Let us confess our sin against God and our neighbor.

People

Almighty God, you love us, but we have not loved you. You call, but we have not listened. We walk away from neighbors in need, wrapped in our own concerns. We condone evil, prejudice, warfare, and greed. God of grace, help us to admit our sin, so that as you come to us in mercy, we may repent, turn to you, and receive forgiveness, through Jesus Christ our Redeemer. Amen.

Celebrant

Almighty God, who forgives all who truly repent, have mercy on you and set you free from sin, strengthen you in goodness, and keep you in eternal life; through Jesus Christ our Lord.

All

Amen.

Sharing the Peace

Celebrant
God makes peace within us.

People
Let us claim it.

Celebrant
God makes peace between us.

People
Let us share it.

Announcements and Offertory

Offertory Sentence

Celebrant
Let us bring before God the offerings of our hearts and our lives, that our hearts may turn to God's love and our lives may witness God's glory.

The Great Thanksgiving

Celebrant
The Lord be with you.

People
And also with you.

Celebrant
Lift up your hearts.

People
We lift them to the Lord.

Celebrant
Let us give thanks to the Lord our God.

People
It is right to give God thanks and praise.

Celebrant
All things are yours, O God of creation,

People
And so we return our gifts of treasure to you.

Celebrant

Blessed are you, O God of creation, through whose goodness we have this bread to offer, which earth has given and human hands have made;

People

May it become for us the bread of life.

Celebrant

Blessed are you, O God of creation, through whose goodness we have this wine to offer, fruit of the vine and work of human hands;

People

May it become for us the cup of blessing.

Celebrant

Receive these gifts, dear God, and accept in them the sacrifice of our selves.

People

In life and in death may we be an offering to you for ever.

Celebrant

We offer you praise and hearts lifted high, O God, by whose Word the heavens and the earth were formed. The power of your love sets aflame each created thing. And though earth's fires will die, you keep the flame of love alive in us and call life out of death into the light that endures forever. Therefore with heaven and earth's host of light and with all who live in the Spirit, we join in the song of your unending greatness:

The Sanctus

All

Holy, holy, holy Lord; God of power and might.
Heaven and earth are filled with your glory.
Hosanna in the highest!
Blessed is the One who comes in the name of the Lord.
Hosanna in the highest!

The Eucharistic Prayer

Celebrant

Blessed are you, O God, for the great day of salvation
prepared from the beginning of the world, when Christ,
though rejected on earth, will be seen by all to be chosen
and precious in your sight. We bless you for Christ, who
carried to the cross sin's destructive powers that all
people might be set free. Through Christ you inspire in us
the hope that earth's forces of darkness will be scattered,
and angels of glory and principalities of light will bring a
new heaven and a new earth.

On the night when he was betrayed, Jesus took
bread, and having blessed it, broke the bread, and gave it
to his disciples, saying: "Take, eat; this is my body which
is broken for you. Do this in remembrance of me." In the
same way Jesus took wine, and having given thanks for
it, gave the cup to his disciples, saying: "This cup is the
new covenant in my blood. Do this, as often as you drink
it, in remembrance of me."

People

Remembering his eternal self-giving, we proclaim the
mystery of Christ among us. Made one with him and one
with each other, we offer these gifts and with them
ourselves, a single, holy living sacrifice.

Celebrant

Bless us with your Holy Spirit, O God, and bless this
bread and wine, that through them we may be made
strong again with the strength that only you supply. May
our inner selves be nourished that in the outward things
of life we may follow the way of Christ and grow more
and more into your love; through Christ, by whom, with
whom, and in whom, in the unity of the Holy Spirit, all
glory and honor is yours, almighty God, for ever and
ever.

All

    Amen.

The Lord's Prayer

Celebrant

    As our Savior Christ has taught us, we now pray:

All

    Our Father in heaven, hallowed be your Name,
        your kingdom come, your will be done,
        on earth as in heaven.
    Give us today our daily bread.
    Forgive us our sins
        as we forgive those who sin against us.
    Save us from the time of trial, and deliver us from evil.
    For the kingdom, the power,
        and the glory are yours, now and forever. Amen.

The Breaking of the Bread

Celebrant

    Warm and loving God, you invite us to your table;

People

    Nourish us with the cup of life and the bread of heaven.

Celebrant

    These are the gifts of God for the people of God.

The Sharing of a Holy Meal

The Closing Prayers

Celebrant

    Let us pray.

All

    O God, in love you have called us to be your people and
    with love you have given us this bread and wine; may this
    holy meal fill us with the flame of your love, that
    renewed and warmed in the comfort of your Holy Spirit,

we may go forth into the world to serve your people; in
the name of God, Creator, Redeemer, and Sanctifier.
Amen.

Celebrant

Lord of all light, as we go forth into the world,
we extinguish the lights that here represent
the presence of the Holy in our midst,

People

But we will carry the light in our hearts,
and we pray that as we go about
our work in the world,
we will shine with the love of God. Amen.

The Blessing

Celebrant

In darkness and in light, as we sleep and when we wake,
in rest and in work, in sadness and in joy,
may we be aware of your holy presence
and mindful of your faithful love.
And the blessing of God, Father, Son, and Holy Spirit,
be upon you and remain with you always.

All

Amen.

The Dismissal

Deacon or Celebrant

Let us go forth into the world to share the love of God.

People

Thanks be to God!

**A Celebration of the Holy Eucharist
in the Celtic Tradition
for the Season after Pentecost:
The Wind of the Holy Spirit**

Opening Words
Celebrant
   The God of love is with us.
People
   The Spirit of love is in us.
Celebrant
   Blessed is the Holy Spirit, the breath of God.
People
   Let the winds and all creation praise you.

The Lighting of the Three Lights
Celebrant
   We will light a light in the name of the Maker –
People
   God who breathed life into all creation.
Celebrant
   We will light a light in the name of Christ –
People
   Jesus who taught of the love that flows in all.
Celebrant
   We will light a light in the name of the Spirit   –
People
   The Holy One embracing us like the wind.

Opening Prayer
Celebrant
   The Lord of the four winds be with you.
People
   And also with you.

Celebrant

Let us pray.

Almighty and eternal God, to you our hearts are open and our inmost desires known. We cannot hide our most intimate secrets from you. Be present at all times in our thoughts and hearts and purify them with your Holy Spirit, so that we may love you with the love of the Spirit and praise your name with humility and joy; through Christ our Lord.

All

Amen.

OR

Celebrant

Holy Spirit, giver of life, creative breath of God through whom this world was breathed into existence and is sustained; blow with power and wisdom through our lives and infuse us with your indwelling, that we may be empowered and open to bring your kingdom to earth; through Christ our Lord.

All

Amen.

A Hymn of Praise

Celebrant

God breathes life into creation.
Let us praise the God of all breath, of all creation!
O God, our Strength,

People

We praise you for your power.

Celebrant

O God, our Shield,

People

We praise you for your protection.

Celebrant
   O God, our Comfort,
People
   We praise you for your solace.
Celebrant
   O God, our Inspiration,
People
   We praise you for your renewal.
Celebrant
   O God, our Life,
People
   We praise you for your grace.
Celebrant
   O God of all,
People
   We praise you for your love.
   Glory to the God of all! Glory forever! Amen.

A Prayer for the Day
Celebrant
   The Lord be with you.
People
   And also with you.
Celebrant
   Let us pray.
<Here is read a prayer or collect selected for the day.>

The First Reading
<After the reading, the people respond>
   Thanks be to God.

A Psalm or Poem

The Second Reading *<The people respond>*
   Thanks be to God.

<A hymn or anthem or "Alleluia" may be sung here.>

The Gospel
Deacon or Celebrant
> The Holy Gospel of our Lord Jesus Christ . . .

People
> Glory to you, Lord Christ.

<Here the Gospel is read, the people facing the reader.>
Deacon or Celebrant
> The Gospel of the Lord.

People
> Praise to you, Lord Christ.

The Sermon

An Affirmation of Faith
Celebrant
> Let us join in affirming our faith in God.

All
> Our God is the God of all humanity,
>> of heaven and earth, of the seas and the rivers,
>> of the sun and the moon, and all the stars,
>
> God of the highest mountains and of the lowest valleys,
>> over heaven, in heaven, and under heaven.
>
> God is present in all things in heaven and earth and seas,
>> inspires all things, brings life to all things,
>> is over all things and supports all things.
>
> God makes the light of the sun to shine,
>> and surrounds the moon and stars,
>> brings water to the deserts
>> and places dry islands in the sea.
>
> God's Son lives as God lives, eternal and holy.
> The Holy Spirit breathes in the Father and the Son,
>> and the Holy Spirit lives in God the Christ.
>
> And God is forever. Amen.

The Prayers of the People

Celebrant

We now pray for the needs of all people throughout the world, remembering that we are God's people and the hand of love on earth. Let us pray.

Intercessor

Blessed are you, O God, for your breath at the heart of creation from which the winds of joy and gladness come forth;

People

For the gentle breezes that bring coolness and refreshment.

Intercessor

As we give thanks for the gift of life and for the comfort we receive in your holy presence, we pray for those places in our world and our lives where there is no joy or comfort;

People

For communities in ruins and war-torn people and nations; for those held captive physically or emotionally;

Intercessor

For those who are weary or weakened by troubles

People

And those who are dying and frightened;

Intercessor

For the sick and the suffering, especially those we now name.

<Pause for additional prayers.>

For the departed and those who mourn.

<Pause for additional prayers.>

We ask your comfort and your holy presence, Lord,

People

For all people, for our loved ones and for ourselves.

Intercessor

We pray to you, O God, asking that we may know your breath of love within us and that our lives may be a witness to that love and to your glory.

Celebrant

May God guide us with wisdom, help us with mercy, bless us with grace, and empower us with love; for the sake of Jesus Christ.

All

Amen.

Confession and Forgiveness

Deacon or Celebrant

We gather together in search of wholeness, but our brokenness separates us from God and from one another. Let us confess our sin against God and our neighbor.

All

Almighty God, you love us, but we have not loved you. You call, but we have not listened. We walk away from neighbors in need, wrapped in our own concerns. We condone evil, prejudice, warfare, and greed. God of grace, help us to admit our sin, so that we may repent, turn to you, and receive forgiveness, through Jesus Christ our Redeemer. Amen.

Celebrant

Almighty God, who forgives all who truly repent, have mercy on you and set you free from sin, strengthen you in goodness, and keep you in eternal life; through Jesus Christ our Lord.

All

Amen.

Sharing the Peace

Celebrant

God makes peace within us.

People

Let us claim it.

Celebrant

God makes peace between us.

People

Let us share it.

Announcements and Offertory

The Great Thanksgiving

Celebrant

The Lord be with you.

People

And also with you.

Celebrant

Lift up your hearts.

People

We lift them to the Lord.

Celebrant

Let us give thanks to the Lord our God.

People

It is right to give God thanks and praise.

Celebrant

All things are yours, O God of creation,

People

And so we return our gifts of treasure to you.

Celebrant

Blessed are you, O God of creation, through whose goodness we have this bread to offer, which earth has given and human hands have made;

People

May it become for us the bread of life.

Celebrant

Blessed are you, O God of creation, through whose goodness we have this wine to offer, fruit of the vine and work of human hands;

People

May it become for us the cup of blessing.

Celebrant

Receive these gifts, dear God, and accept in them the sacrifice of our selves.

People

In life and in death may we be an offering to you for ever.

Celebrant

We offer you praise and hearts lifted high, O God. You breathe into us your Spirit, and by the blowing of the gentle breeze, you remind us of the constancy of your loving presence. Your glory is in the breath of each created thing, and through your creation we see the holiness and wonder of your being. And so with all the hosts of heaven and earth, with the wind that howls and the gentle breeze that soothes, we join in the praises of your unending greatness:

The Sanctus

All

Holy, holy, holy Lord; God of power and might.
    Heaven and earth are filled with your glory.
    Hosanna in the highest!
Blessed is the One who comes in the name of the Lord.
    Hosanna in the highest!

The Eucharistic Prayer

Celebrant

Blessed are you, O God, for the great day of salvation prepared from the beginning of the world, when Christ, though rejected on earth, will be seen by all to be chosen and precious in your sight. We bless you for Christ who carried sin's destructive powers to the cross that all people might be set free. Through Christ you inspire in us the hope that earth's forces of darkness will be scattered, and angels of glory and principalities of light will bring a new heaven and a new earth.

Just as prophets long before Christ had spoken of the sufferings that would be his, so Jesus on the night when he was betrayed took bread, and having blessed it, he broke the bread, and gave it to his disciples, saying: "Take, eat; this is my body which is broken for you. Do this in remembrance of me." In the same way he took wine, and having given thanks for it, he gave the cup to his disciples, saying: "This cup is the new covenant in my blood. Do this, as often as you drink it, in remembrance of me."

People

Remembering his eternal self-giving, we proclaim the mystery of Christ among us. Made one with him and one with each other, we offer these gifts and with them ourselves, a single, holy living sacrifice.

Celebrant

Bless us with your Holy Spirit, O God, and bless this bread and this wine, that through them we may be made strong again with the strength that only you supply. May our inner selves be nourished that in the outward things of life we may follow the way of Christ and grow more and more into salvation; through Christ, by whom, with whom, and in whom, in the unity of the Holy Spirit, all glory and honor is yours, almighty God, world without end.

All

Amen.

The Lord's Prayer

Celebrant

As our Savior Christ has taught us, we now pray:

All

Our Father in heaven, hallowed be your Name,
  your kingdom come, your will be done,
  on earth as in heaven.
Give us today our daily bread.
Forgive us our sins
  as we forgive those who sin against us.
Save us from the time of trial, and deliver us from evil.
For the kingdom, the power,
  and the glory are yours, now and forever. Amen.

The Breaking of the Bread

Celebrant

The Bread of heaven is broken for the life of the world.

People

The Cup of love is shared with all who seek God. Amen.

The Sharing of a Holy Meal

The Closing Prayers

Celebrant

Let us pray.

All

O God, in love you have called us to be your people and in love you have given us this bread and wine; may this holy meal refresh us as a gentle and steady breeze, that renewed in your Holy Spirit, we may go forth into the world to serve your people; in the name of God, who is Love. Amen.

Celebrant

Lord of all light, as we go forth into the world,
  we extinguish the lights that here represent

the presence of the Holy in our midst,

People

But we will carry the light in our hearts,
and we pray that as we go about
our work in the world,
we will shine with the love of God. Amen.

The Blessing

Celebrant

The power and peace of the Presence protect you.
The grace and goodness of the saints inspire you.
The good and gracious God go with you
and keep you always.
And the blessing of God almighty,
Father, Son and Holy Spirit
be with you now and for ever.

All

Amen.

The Dismissal

Celebrant

Let us go forth into the world rejoicing
in the power of the Spirit.

People

Thanks be to God!

**A Celebration of the Holy Eucharist
in the Celtic Tradition
for All Saints Sunday:
A Celebration of the Baptismal Fellowship of the Saints**

Opening Words
Celebrant
    The God of love is with us.
People
    The Spirit of love is in us.
Celebrant
    Blessed are you in the heights and the depths, O God.
People
    Let the eternal waters praise you.
    Let the seas and the rivers sing your glory.

The Lighting of the Three Lights
Celebrant
    We will light a light in the name of the Maker –
People
    God who moved over the face of the waters.
Celebrant
    We will light a light in the name of Christ –
People
    Jesus who was baptized in the water of the Jordan.
Celebrant
    We will light a light in the name of the Spirit –
People
    The Holy One who cleanses and refreshes us
        as the cool spring water.

Opening Prayer
Celebrant
    Let us pray.
    Almighty and eternal God, to you our hearts are open

and our inmost desires are known. We cannot hide our most intimate secrets from you. We ask you to be present at all times in our thoughts and our hearts and to purify them, so that we may love you with the love of the Spirit and praise your name with humility and joy; through Christ our Lord.

All

Amen.

A Hymn of Praise

Celebrant

Let us praise the God of all things.

How wonderful, O Lord, are the works of your hands!

People

The heavens declare your glory.

Celebrant

In your love you have given us power,

People

Power to behold the beauty of your world
in all its splendor.

Celebrant

The sun and the stars, the valleys and the hills,

People

The rivers and lakes all reveal your presence.

Celebrant

The roaring breakers of the sea tell
of your awesome might.

People

The gentle babble of a brook celebrates
the comfort of your love.

Celebrant

The waters of baptism mark our covenant with you.

People

Glory to our life-giving God!

May we give thanks for all his works,

praise him in all we do,
and share his love with the communion of saints.

A Prayer for the Day
Celebrant
    The Lord be with you.
People
    And also with you.
Celebrant
    Let us pray.
<Here is read a prayer or collect selected for the day.>

The First Reading
<After the reading, the people respond>
    Thanks be to God.

A Psalm or Poem

The Second Reading
<After the reading, the people respond>
    Thanks be to God.

<A hymn or anthem or "Alleluia" may be sung here.>

The Gospel
Deacon or Celebrant
    The Holy Gospel of our Lord Jesus Christ . . .
People
    Glory to you, Lord Christ.
<Here the Gospel is read, the people facing the reader.>
Deacon or Celebrant
    The Gospel of the Lord.
People
    Praise to you, Lord Christ.

The Sermon

The Affirmation of Faith: The Baptismal Covenant
Celebrant
  Let us stand and, like the saints before us, reaffirm our
  baptismal covenant. Do you believe in God the Father?
People
  I believe in God, the Father almighty, creator of heaven
  and earth.
Celebrant
  Do you believe in Jesus Christ, the Son of God?
People
  I believe in Jesus Christ, his only Son, our Lord. He was
  conceived by the power of the Holy Spirit and born of the
  Virgin Mary. He suffered under Pontius Pilate, was
  crucified, died, and was buried. He descended to the
  dead. On the third day he rose again. He ascended into
  heaven, and is seated at the right hand of the Father. He
  will come again to judge the living and the dead.
Celebrant
  Do you believe in God the Holy Spirit?
People
  I believe in the Holy Spirit, the holy Catholic Church, the
  communion of saints, the forgiveness of sins, the
  resurrection of the body, and the life everlasting.
Celebrant
  Will you continue in the apostles' teaching and
  fellowship, in the breaking of bread, and in the prayers?
People
  I will, with God's help.
Celebrant
  Will you persevere in resisting evil, and, whenever you
  fall into sin, repent and return to the Lord?
People
  I will, with God's help.

Celebrant

Will you proclaim by word and example the Good News of God in Christ?

People

I will, with God's help.

Celebrant

Will you seek and serve Christ in all persons, loving your neighbor as yourself?

People

I will, with God's help.

Celebrant

Will you strive for justice and peace among all people, and respect the dignity of every human being?

People

I will, with God's help.

Celebrant

May Almighty God, the Father of our Lord Jesus Christ, who has given us a new birth by water and the Holy Spirit, and bestowed upon us the forgiveness of sins, keep us in eternal life by his grace in Christ Jesus our Lord.

All

Amen.

The Prayers of the People

Celebrant

We pray now for the needs of all people throughout the world, remembering that, following the example of the saints before us, we are God's hands in the world. Let us pray.

Intercessor

We pray for the world and for the leaders of the nations,

People

That, like the saints, they may be bold in their search for peace and justice.

Intercessor

We pray for the Church and for its leaders and people,

People

That we may be ever ready to share the Gospel and to serve our neighbors.

Intercessor

We pray for all of us gathered here in worship together,

People

That we may recognize each other as saints of God and keepers of the faith.

Intercessor

We pray for the earth and its generous bounty, and for our stewardship of its resources,

People

That we may have the courage to change our lives in order to ensure its future.

Intercessor

We pray for those who suffer from famine, poverty, persecution, danger, loneliness, or grief,

People

That they may know the certainty of your love and find comfort in you.

<Pause for additional prayers>

Intercessor

We pray for those who are sick, injured or in pain,

People

That those who minister to them may help ease their burden through God's love.

<Pause for additional prayers>

Intercessor

We pray for all who have died and are with the communion of saints,

People

That all may be one with you, and that all the saints may be witnesses to your eternal glory.

<Pause for additional prayers>
Celebrant
   Loving God, hear our prayers on behalf of all those in
   need. In your great mercy, comfort them and bring them
   hope. For you alone know our needs, and you alone can
   be our refuge in the time of trouble. We pray through
   Jesus Christ, our Lord. Amen.

Sharing the Peace
Celebrant
   God makes peace within us.
People
   Let us claim it.
Celebrant
   God makes peace between us.
People
   Let us share it.

Announcements and Offertory

The Great Thanksgiving
Celebrant
   The Lord be with you.
People
   And also with you.
Celebrant
   Lift up your hearts.
People
   We lift them to the Lord.
Celebrant
   Let us give thanks to the Lord our God.
People
   It is right to give God thanks and praise.
Celebrant
   All things are yours, O God of creation,

People

And so we return our gifts of treasure to you.

Celebrant

Blessed are you, O God of creation, through whose goodness we have this bread to offer, which earth has given and human hands have made;

People

May it become for us the bread of life.

Celebrant

Blessed are you, O God of creation, through whose goodness we have this wine to offer, fruit of the vine and work of human hands;

People

May it become for us the cup of blessing.

Celebrant

Receive these gifts, dear God, and accept in them the sacrifice of our selves.

People

In life and in death may we be an offering to you for ever.

Celebrant

We offer you praise and hearts lifted high, O God, by whose Word the heavens were formed and the earth was brought forth from the waters. The reflection of your glory shines in each created thing. And though earth's flowering fades, you plant within us imperishable seeds for our salvation and call life out of death into the light that endures forever. And so with heaven and earth's host of light, with the sainted women and men of every nation, and with those who now live in the Spirit, we join in the song of your unending greatness:

The Sanctus

All

Holy, holy, holy Lord; God of power and might.
Heaven and earth are filled with your glory.

Hosanna in the highest!
Blessed is the One who comes in the name of the Lord.
Hosanna in the highest!

The Eucharistic Prayer

Celebrant

Blessed are you, O God, for the great day of salvation prepared from the beginning of the world, when Christ, though rejected on earth, will be seen by all to be chosen and precious in your sight. We bless you for Christ, who carried to the cross sin's destructive powers that all people might be set free. Through Christ you inspire the hope that earth's forces of darkness will be scattered and angels of glory and principalities of light will bring a new heaven and a new earth. Knowing of the sufferings that would be his, Jesus, on the night when he was betrayed, took bread. And, having blessed it, he broke the bread, and gave it to his disciples, saying: "Take, eat; this is my body which is broken for you. Do this in remembrance of me." In the same way he took wine and, having given thanks for it, he gave the cup to his disciples, saying: "This cup is the new covenant in my blood. Do this, as often as you drink it, in remembrance of me."

People

Remembering his eternal self-giving, we proclaim the mystery of Christ among us. Made one with him and one with each other, we offer these gifts and with them ourselves, a single, holy, living sacrifice.

Celebrant

Bless us with your Holy Spirit, O God, and bless this bread and wine, that through them we may be made strong again with the strength that only you supply. May our inner selves be nourished that in the outward things of life we may follow the way of Christ and grow more and more into salvation. We ask this through Christ, by

whom, with whom, and in whom, in the unity of the Holy
Spirit, all glory and honor is yours, almighty God, for ever
and ever.
All
Amen.

The Lord's Prayer
Celebrant
As our Savior Christ has taught us, we now pray:
All
Our Father in heaven, hallowed be your Name,
your kingdom come, your will be done,
on earth as in heaven.
Give us today our daily bread.
Forgive us our sins
as we forgive those who sin against us.
Save us from the time of trial, and deliver us from evil.
For the kingdom, the power,
and the glory are yours, now and forever. Amen.

The Breaking of the Bread
Celebrant
The Bread of heaven is broken for the life of the world.

The Sharing of a Holy Meal

The Closing Prayers
Celebrant
Let us stand and join in thanking God for this holy meal.
All
O God, we thank you for the gift of this bread and wine
that have served here as earthly reminders
of your heavenly love.
We pray now that as the waters of the earth
purify your creation,

you will cleanse us with your Holy Spirit
as gentle and pure as the cool spring water,
that, renewed by this holy meal,
we may go forth into the world to serve your people;
    in the name of God,
    Creator, Redeemer, and Sanctifier. Amen.
Celebrant
Lord of all light, as we go forth into the world,
    we extinguish the lights that here represent
    the presence of the Holy in our midst,
People
But we will carry the light in our hearts,
    and we pray that as we go about
    our work in the world,
    we will shine with the love of God. Amen.

The Blessing
Celebrant
Let us now go forth with the grace of God,
    the gentleness of Jesus,
    the comfort of the Holy Spirit,
    the courage of the saints,
    and the songs of angels in our hearts
And may the blessing of God,
    Father, Son and Holy Spirit,
    be with you now and always.
All
Amen.

The Dismissal
Celebrant
Let us go forth into the world,
    rejoicing in the power of the Spirit.
People
Thanks be to God!

Notes

All material excerpted from the works of others is incorporated here with the permission of the author or other copyright holder. Every effort has been made to obtain permission for the reprinting of each prayer, acclamation or other liturgical text (or adaptation thereof) herein included. We apologize for any errors in this process.

Separate source notes are not given for some common liturgical texts that can be found (among other places) in *The Book of Common Prayer.* This includes the Lord's Prayer (p . 364 – contemporary version) and the dismissal (p. 366). The prayers for each Sunday can be found on pp. 211-236. The responses to the readings are on pp. 357-358.

Any prayer or liturgical element not otherwise credited was written by the author. If original prayers resemble those created by others, it is not intentional but arises from following a Celtic theology and a Celtic style.

Sources for the Advent liturgy
Opening Prayer
    Adapted from the Collect for Purity, *The Book of Common Prayer* (New York: Church Publishing, 1979), p. 355
Hymn of Praise
    "The Song of Mary," *The Book of Common Prayer*, pp. 91-92
Affirmation
    The Iona Community, *Iona Abbey Worship Book* (Glasgow: Wild Goose Publications, 2001), pp. 38-39
Prayers of the People
    Diana Macalintal, Roman Catholic Diocese of San Jose, Intercessions for December 24, 2006
Peace
    The New Women Included: A Book of Services and Prayers

St. Hilda Community (London: SPCK, 1996), p. 55
Great Thanksgiving and Eucharistic Prayer
    Adapted from J. Philip Newell, *An Earthful of Glory*
    (London: SPCK, 1996), pp. 99-102
Blessing
    Adapted from David Adam, *The Rhythm of Life: Celtic
    Daily Prayer* (Harrisburg, PA: Morehouse Publishing,
    1996), p. 54

Sources for the Nativity liturgy
Hymn of Praise
    Newell, *Earthful of Glory*, p. 140
Affirmation
    Iona Abbey Worship Book, pp. 38-39
Prayers of the People
    Adapted from Adam, *Rhythm of Life*, p. 47
Peace
    The New Women Included, p. 55
Great Thanksgiving and Eucharistic Prayer
    Adapted from Newell, *Earthful of Glory*, pp. 78-81
Blessing
    Adapted from Adam, *Rhythm of Life*, p. 54

Sources for the Epiphany liturgy
Hymn of Praise
    Adapted from Adam, *The Rhythm of Life*, p. 55
    (adapted from an ancient Celtic prayer)
Canticle of Light
    "The Third Song of Isaiah," *The Book of Common Prayer*,
    p. 87
Affirmation
    Iona Abbey Worship Book, pp. 38-39
Prayers of the People
    Adapted from *Book of Common Worship* (Louisville, KY:
    Westminster John Knox Press, 1993) pp. 109-111

Confession
    Book of Common Worship, p. 193
Peace
    The New Women Included, p. 55
Great Thanksgiving and Eucharistic Prayer
    Adapted from Newell, *Earthful of Glory*, pp. 78-81

Sources for the Lent liturgy
Penitential Litany
    Adapted from Adam, *Rhythm of Life*, p. 98
Confession
    Book of Common Worship, p. 236
Affirmation
    Adapted from Tirechan's Creed from *The Patrician Texts
    the Book of Armagh*, Ludwig Bieler, ed. (Dublin:
    Governing Board of the School of Celtic Studies of the
    Dublin Institute for Advanced Studies, 1979), p. 143
Prayers of the People
    Adapted from Newell, *Earthful of Glory*, p. 51
Peace
    The New Women Included, p. 55
Great Thanksgiving, Eucharistic Prayer, and Breaking of
Bread
    Adapted from J. Philip Newell, *A Celtic Mass for
    Peace* (Guarnaccia Music, 2009)

Sources for Easter liturgy
Opening Prayer
    Adapted from prayer "For Knowledge of God's Creation,"
    The Book of Common Prayer, p. 827
Hymn of Praise
    Adapted from J. Philip Newell, *Celtic Treasure: Daily
    Scriptures and Prayer* (Grand Rapids, MI: Eerdmans,
    2005) pp. 5, 9, 13, 17, 21 and 25.

Affirmation
    Adapted from *The Patrician Texts*, p. 143
Peace
    The New Women Included, p. 55
Great Thanksgiving and Eucharistic Prayer
    Adapted from Newell, *Earthful of Glory* pp. 85-88

Sources for the Pentecost liturgy (fire theme)
Opening Prayer
    Adapted from the Collect for Purity, *The Book of Common Prayer*, p. 355
Affirmation
    Adapted from *The Patrician Texts*, p. 143
Prayers of the People
    Adapted from *Book of Common Worship*, pp. 109-111
Confession
    Adapted from *Book of Common Worship*, p. 89
Peace
    The New Women Included, p. 55
Great Thanksgiving and Eucharistic Prayer
    Adapted from Newell, *Earthful of Glory*, pp. 85-88

Sources for the Pentecost liturgy (wind theme)
Opening Prayer
    Adapted from the Collect for Purity, *The Book of Common Prayer*, p. 355
Affirmation
    Adapted from *The Patrician Texts*, p. 143
Prayers of the People
    Adapted from Newell, *Earthful of Glory*, p. 38
Confession
    Adapted from *Book of Common Worship*, p. 89
Peace
    The New Women Included, p. 55

Great Thanksgiving and Eucharistic Prayer
  Adapted from Newell, *Earthful of Glory*, pp. 85-88
Blessing
  Adam, *Rhythm of Life,* p. 118

Sources for the All Saints liturgy (water theme)
Opening Words
  Adapted from J. Philip Newell, *Celtic Treasure*, p. 4
Opening Prayer
  Adapted from the Collect for Purity, *The Book of Common Prayer*, p. 355
Hymn of Praise
  Adapted from Adam, *Rhythm of Life*, pp. 29-30
Affirmation
  The Baptismal Covenant, *The Book of Common Prayer*, pp. 304-305
Peace
  The New Women Included, p. 55
Great Thanksgiving and Eucharistic Prayer
  Adapted from Newell, *Earthful of Glory*, pp. 85-88

Bibliography

David Adam, *The Rhythm of Life: Celtic Daily Prayer* (Morehouse Publishing,1996)

David Adam, *The Edge of Glory: Prayers in the Celtic Tradition* (Triangle/SPCK, 1985)

Ludwig Bieler, editor The Patrician Texts in the Book of Armagh (Dublin: Dublin Institute for Advanced Studies, 1979)

The Book of Common Prayer (New York: Seabury Press, 1979)

The Book of Common Worship (Louisville, KY: Westminster John Knox Press, 1993)

Celebrate God's Presence: A Book of Services for the United Church of Canada (Toronto: United Church Publishing House, 2000)

Daily Readings from Prayers and Praises in the Celtic Tradition, edited by A. M. Allchin and Esther de Waal (Springfield, IL: Templegate, 1987)

Oliver Davies and Fiona Bowie, *Celtic Christian Spirituality: An Anthology of Medieval and Modern Sources* (New York: Continuum, 1995)

Iona Community, *Iona Abbey Worship Book* (Glasgow: Wild Goose Worship Group, 2001)

J. Philip Newell, *An Earthful of Glory: Biblical prayers, liturgies, and meditations* (SPCK, 1996)

J. Philip Newell, *Celtic Treasure: Daily Scriptures and Prayer* (Eerdmans, 2005)

J. Philip Newell, *A Celtic Mass for Peace: Songs from the Earth* (Guarnaccia Music, 2009)

Brendan O'Malley, editor and compiler, *A Celtic Primer: The Complete Celtic Worship Resource and Collection* (Morehouse, 2002)

The St. Hilda Community, *The New Women Included: A Book of Services and Prayers* (SPCK, 1996)

Ray Simpson, *Celtic Worship Through the Year* (London: Hodder & Stoughton, 1997)

Wild Goose Worship Group, *A Wee Worship Book: Fourth incarnation* (Chicago: GIA Publications, 1999)

Printed in Great Britain
by Amazon